ISBN 978-0-260-05028-1
PIBN 10924538

This book is a reproduction of an important historical work. Forgotten Books uses state-of-the-art technology to digitally reconstruct the work, preserving the original format whilst repairing imperfections present in the aged copy. In rare cases, an imperfection in the original, such as a blemish or missing page, may be replicated in our edition. We do, however, repair the vast majority of imperfections successfully; any imperfections that remain are intentionally left to preserve the state of such historical works.

THIS is just another Carontawan, the twelfth edition of the "Little Town on the Hill." It will recall to your mind memories of Mansfield State. It will help bind you closer to the traditions of your Alma Mater. As your days have been pleasant; as your friendship, lasting; as your work, profitable; so will the Carontawan of 1929 be treasured by you.

*With sentiments too deep-rooted to be trans-
lated into words; with all appreciation for past
services to our College; with the sincere respect
of a Mansfield class to a faculty member; and
with the affection of friend to friend,
the Senior Class of 1929 dedicate this,
"Our Carontawan,"
to*

Will George Butler

In Memoriam.

C. J. Beach
President of Trustees

Elva Nyenhuis
Class of 1929

The Campus

For a man's house is his castle, et domus
sua cuique tutissimum refugium

Better build schoolrooms for "the boy"
Than cells and gibbets for "the man"

All the charms of all the Muses
often flowering in a lonely world

Low drooping pine-boughs, winter-weighed

Administration

Wm. R. Straughn, Ph. D., Principal

The Faculty

Administration

Deceased

WILLIAM R. STRAUGHN, Ph. D., Principal. Ethics. Baltimore City College; Johns Hopkins University; University of Kansas.

Deceased

ARTHUR T. BELKNAP, M. A., S. T. B., D. D. Dean of Instruction; English. Brown University; Newton Theological Institution; Harvard University; Sioux Falls College.

MILDRED FISCHER, B. S., M. A. Dean of Women. Philadelphia Normal; University of Pennsylvania; Columbia University.

CLIFFORD P. BALCH, A. B. Dean of Men; History. Mansfield State Normal; Franklin and Marshall College; University of Pennsylvania; Bucknell.

MRS. LILLIAN McKINNEY. Dietitian and Instructor of Nutrition. Albany Hospital; University of Pittsburgh; University of Chicago.

Deceased

MARGARET HUTCHESON. Bursar. Mansfield State.

HELEN R. JUPENLAZ. Secretary to Principal. Mansfield State; Meeker's; Palmer School of Business.

GUSSIE JUPENLAZ. Office Clerk. Mansfield State; Meeker's.

EDNA L. HEWSON. Secretary to Dean. New York State Normal; Gregg School.

MANDERVILLE BARTLE. Bookroom Clerk. Mansfield State; New York University.

Deceased

CARRIE E. PIERSON. Matron. Mechanics Institute of Rochester.

F. E. BROOKS. Superintendent of Grounds and Buildings.

College

GEORGE W. CASS, A. M. Social Sciences, Mansfield State; Dickinson College.

IRVING T. CHATTERTON, B. S., M. A.. Oral Expression. Boston University.

CORNELIA B. CORNISH, B. S. Geography and Social Sciences. Columbia.

EDWARD H. CORNISH, B. A. Geography and Science. Cornell University.

JOHN W. CURE, Ph. B., Ed. M. English. Bucknell University; Harvard University.

ALICE HORTON DOANE, A. B. Latin; English. Mansfield State; Columbia.

17

JOHN H. DOANE, M. D. Physician; Health Education. Mansfield State; Medico Chirurgical College; Philadelphia General Hospital; Columbia.

STELLA T. DOANE. Librarian. Mansfield State; Drexel; University of Pennsylvania; Carnegie Library School.

Deceased
ISAAC DOUGHTON, M. A., Ph. D. Education. Harvard University; University of Pennsylvania.

EMMA A. GILLETTE, A. B., M. A. German; English. Alleghany College; Columbia.

CHARLES S. GILBERT, B. Ped. Penmanship. University of Nebraska; Palmer School of Penmanship; Zanerian College of Penmanship.

HERBERT GRANT, M. S. Chemistry and Physics. Cornell and Columbia Universities.

ANNA E. HARKNESS. Nurse. Chautauqua School; Private Nurse (Fifteen years).

DOROTHY F. HUTCHINSON, B. S. Psychology. Mansfield State; University of Pennsylvana.

ANNA MARIE LOVE., B. S. Health Education. Randolph Macon College; University of Michigan; Columbia University.

SARAH MAC DONALD, A. B. Assistant Librarian. Randolph Macon Woman's College; Carnegie Library School.

Deceased
GEORGE H. McNAIR, Ph. D. Educational Mathematics. New York University; People's National University.

HERBERT E. MANSER, B. S., A. M. French; Psychology. Columbia University.

ELIZABETH GLASS MARSHALL, B. A., M. A., Ph. D. English. University of Virginia; University of Kentucky; Oxford University, England.

KIMBLE G. MARVIN, B. S. Health Education; Coach. Lafayette; New York University.

JAMES G. MORGAN, Ph. B. Education. Muhlenberg College; New York University; University of Michigan; University of Pennsylvania.

EDWARD C. RUSSELL, B. S. Football Coach. Mansfield State; University of Pennsylvania.

Deceased
GEORGE B. STRAIT, B. S. Biology. Mansfield State; Syracuse University.

Deceased
O. L. WARREN, Ped. D. Education. University of Michigan; Alfred University.

LAURA A. WHEELER. Art. Syracuse University.

Training School

GEORGE A. RETAN, B. F., Pd. M., M. A. Director of Training School. Mansfield Normal; New York University.

MYRON E. WEBSTER, L. L. B. Principal of Junior High School. Mansfield Normal; Cornell University.

HUGH W. ALGER, A. B. Supervisor (Geography and Science) Junior High School. West Chester Normal; Bucknell University; Yale University.

BLANCHE ROSS, B. S. Primary Director. Colorado State Normal; Columbia University.

CATHRYN PARKER, A. B. Supervisor of Kindergarten. Kearney Teachers College; University of Nebraska.

DRUCILLA WORTHINGTON, A. B. Supervisor, Grade I. Beloit College; University of Wisconsin.

JESSIE P. WILLETT, A. B. Supervisor, Grade II. Davis Elkins College; Columbia University.

EDNA PUTERBAUGH MARSH, B. S. Supervisor, Grade III. Stroudsburg State Normal; Columbia University.

MARY ELIZABETH RUF, A. B. Supervisor, Grade IV. University of Illinois; Harvard.

ELIZABETH P. STALFORD, B. S. Supervisor, Grade V. Mansfield State Normal; Bucknell University.

MILGRED L. GRIGSBY, B. S. Supervisor, Grade VI. Mansfield State Normal; Bucknell University.

JESSIE GRIGSBY, B. S. Supervisor (Mathematics) Junior High School. Mansfield State Normal; New York University.

MARAGRET O'BRIEN, A. B., M. A. Supervisor (English) Junior High School. Syracuse University; McGill University.

LOUISE BARNHARDT, B. S., M. A. Art Supervisor in Training School. Mansfield State Normal School; Syracuse University; Columbia University.

MARGARET DICK STEADMAN, B. A., B. of Ed. Music Supervisor in Training School. Kearney Teachers College; Iowa State Teachers College.

EDYTHA L. KEENEY, R. N. Training School and Community Nurse. Clifton Springs Sanitarium and Clinic.

WILLIAM CASWELL, B. S. Manual Arts. Mansfield State Teachers College.

Deceased

19

Home Economics

Deceased

LU M. HARTMAN, B. S., M. A. Director of ·Home Economics. Carnegie Institute of Technology; Columbia.

Deceased

SADIE M. SMITH, B. S. Home Economics. University of Chicago; Columbia.

MARYON FARRER, B. S. Home Economics. Mansfield State; Simon's College.

LUCY MARY MALTBY, M. S. Home Economics. Cornell; Iowa State College.

Music Supervisors

Deceased

MRS. GRACE STEADMAN, M. B. in Ed. Director of Music. Kearney State Normal School, Neb.; Cornell University.

WILL GEORGE BUTLER, Mus. Doc. Instructor of Harmony; Orchestra. New York State University Music College; Violin, Ovid Musin, 1898.

CORA A. ATWATER, Mus. B. Voice. Elmira, Cornell University; University Extension Conservatory, Chicago.

DONALD E. BALDWIN. Band and Orchestral Instruments. Mansfield State; New York University.

MARJORIE BROOKS, B. S. Harmony. Institute of Musical Art; New York University.

MARJORIE HOLMES HARTMAN, B. S. Piano. Institute of Musical Art; Mansfield State.

MARGARET LOUISE PAYNE, Mus. B. Piano, Pipe Organ. Syracuse University.

JOHN F. MYERS, A. B. Band; Instructor of Music. Kearney State, Nebraska; Columbia School of Music.

MYRTLE A. MYERS, B. S. in Ed. Piano, Public School Music. Kearney State, Nebraska; University School of Music, Lincoln, Neb.; Hollis Dann School

ELSIE R. PERKINS, Mus. B. Voice. Syracuse University; Chicago Musical College.

LOUISE VROMAN, Mus. B. Public School Music; Training for Piano Teachers. Kearney State, Nebraska; Wisconsin School of Music.

The Classes

Degree Seniors

Education, Home Economics, Music

IRENE ABPLANALP   Old Forge, Pa.
"RENE"

*Rurþan Club; Emersonian Society; Y. W. C. A.;
Baseball* (2); *Hockey* (2) (3).

Breezy and animated with a generous sprinkling
of pep, "Rene" pursues her way undaunted from
teaching assignments to college classes and to social
activities, with the same extraordinary success. She
is distinguished as a gloom subtractor with one of
those natures that adds joy to the sum total of existence.

"Rene's" interpretations of "Cyrano": "Je
t'aime C'est le thœme—Brodez, brodez,"

WILLIAM ALLINGER   Ridgway, Pa.

Quiet and retiring, William is the type of man
you must learn to know. However, despite his retiring disposition, he is far from spineless and those
who know him can well attest to his tempestuous-
ness when aroused. No halfway measures are used
when he starts something. His watch-words are
determination and perseverance.

ALLENE ALLIS   Mansfield, Pa.

*Dramatic Club; Treasurer of Senior Class;
Hockey* (2); *Soccer* (2); *Baseball* (2); *Basketball*
(2); *Athletic Club.*

From downtown we have one of our friendliest
friends. Allene is popular not only for her scholastic ability, but also her strong personality. As proof
of her popularity she was chosen Class Treasurer.
She has always been a loyal supporter of all school
activities.

LEO ALLIS.   Mansfield, Pa.

"SHRIMP"

Varsity Football (1) (2) (3) (4); *Varsity Basketball* (1) (2) (3), *Captain* (4); *"M" Club; Athenaean Literary Society* (1) (2); *President "M" Club* (4); *Y. M. C. A.*

When it comes to campus athletics "Shrimp" is always in the foreground. No "eleven" is complete without the flash and speed of this sturdy "center"; and no "five" is efficient minus his powerful jump. His athletic ability, his genial and hearty disposition have kept him constantly in the limelight.

Leo's interpretation of Spanish would make Don Juan turn over in his grave.

EVELYN ANDERSON   Attleboro, Mass.

Y. W. C. A.; Hiking Club (1); *Secretary Senior Class* (4); *Dramatic Club* (1).

This young lady has that discretion and modesty, without which all knowledge is of little worth. She will never make an ostentations parade of it, because she will rather be intent on acquiring more, than of displaying what she has. "Evie" has been one of the most popular girls Mansfield has known.

HARRY BARTLOW   *Deceased*   New Albany, Pa.

Y. M. C. A.; Intramural Basketball (2) (3).

Harry has had more "ups and downs" with deans and student councils than anyone else in the college. He has majored in all kinds of social activities, and good times. Whenever the fun started Harry was there. Speaking of checkers, we crown him champion of the smoking-room gang.

25

JAMES BENNETT — Mansfield, Pa.
' JIMMIE"

Y. M. C. A. (1) (2) (3) (4).

Voluminous reading in many fields with a keen insight toward the best that is in books is a power within this chap, Bennett.

The giving to friends, colleagues, and opponents, the nicer siftings of the worthwhile materials is a still greater force within Jimmie.

DORIS BENSON — Mansfield, Pa.

J. H. S. Quarterly Board; Soccer (2); *Hockey* (2).

Here abideth abilities, brains, and a sense of sportsmanship. Talk about your fancy steps in dancing, can't you just see her dancing in the gym? Doris is a dark-haired, bright-eyed, sunny-tempered girl. Petite and lovable is she, graceful and sweet. She seems to be made of "cheerful yesterdays and confident tomorrows."

FRANCIS BERDANIER — Knoxville, Pa.

To look at Francis and see him argue you would think that he was another Stephen Douglas. Let him take pro or con on any subject and we are confident that he will emerge topside up. Francis has a heart that fills his chest. For a friend he would do anything—even down to breaking his last "fag" in two. It is inevitable that success will crown his future endeavors.

LEWIS BLY   Mansfield, Pa.

It has been rumored that "Bly" could build new automobiles from old ones when he was three weeks old. Judging from his present and past success, we expect big things from him in the future in the fields of science and teaching.

MARK BURGESS   Forksville, Pa.

A's seem to be his weakness as his instructors can testify. Being a downtown student, we find it hard to become better acquainted with him. He is here and then he is gone. Quiet and unassuming, he takes life as it comes, seldom showing signs of excitement. He thinks and thinks, for he has a brain and the ability to use it.

HOWARD BURR   Canton, Pa.
                "BUCKY"

Varsity Football (1) (2) (3) (4); Basketball Reserves (1) (2); Carontawan (2) (4); Editor of Flashlight (3); Feature Editor (4); Student Council, Vice President (2) (3); President (4); Y. M. C. A. Secretary (2) (3); Treasurer (4); "M" Club; Athenaean Literary Society; Visual Education

In paying tribute to seniors we are prone to paint too well the picture of our regard, with useless words. The mere words we use fool no persons but ourselves. And so in presenting for our hall of remembrance, "Bucky" Burr, we do it because for four years we have found him a constant cause for admiration as a friend, as an athlete, as an executive and as a man who can do well the things he is called upon to do.

27

AGNES CHAMBERLAIN   Mansfield, Pa.

Outdoor Club.

"She sets the cause above renown.
She loves the game beyond the prize.
She honors while she strikes down
The foe that comes with fearless eye.
She's merry all the livelong day,
She loves to work and loves to play.
She counts the life of battle good
And binds the earth in brotherhood."

MAURICE CRUTTENDEN   Mansfield, Pa.

Glee Club (1) (2) (3); *Tennis Teams* (3) (4); *Y. M. C. A.* (1) (2) (3); *Emersonian Literary Society* (4).

"Cruttenden" is the slogan of the boys on the hill when in doubt. It has taken place of the famous slogan, "Ask dad." Maurice is about average physically, but intelligently he is more than huge. Yes, indeed, nothing pleases him more than to wrestle with a difficult problem, especially one for which no one has yet found a solution. Coupled with this he has a sense of humor; plus a quiet reserve which makes him doubly interesting.

J. BRIT DAVIS   Kingston, Pa.
"BRIT"

Freshman Treasurer (1); *Soph Vice President* (2); *Art Club President* (2); *Football Reserves* (1); *Y. M. C. A. Vice President* (3); *General Secretary* (4); *Football Manager* (3); *Flashlight Editor* (2); *Staff* (3) (4); *Carontawan Editor* (3); *Athletic Editor* (4); *Senior Class President* (4); *Student Council* (3) (4).

Few men have had their names more blazoned across the pages of college life than this young man. The list of activities above gives you some idea of how busy "Brit's" four years have been.

Despite these many honors, he remains modest and unassuming, a forceful speaking gentleman. Scholastically "Brit" grades well and his quality of always fulfilling his obligations makes him universally liked.

28

BERNICE DECKER   Clarks Summit, Pa.

Domicilian Club; Y. W. C. A.; Athenacan Literary Society; Glee Club.

Bernice is a true friend. "To act the part of a true friend requires more conscientious feeling than to fill with credit any other station or capacity in social life." Bernice is capable of great accomplishments.

DOROTHY M. DEMER   Hallstead, Pa.

"DOTTIE"

Rurban Club; Outdoor Club; Y. W. C. A.

School Days, School Days,
Dear old Mansfield School Days,
Latin and French and English, too,
That is just what "Dot" likes to do,
You'd be surprised if you only knew
Just how much fun "Dot" likes, too,
Kind-hearted, true, and loafing taboo.
There sure is a lot she can do.

ALFORD DIBBLE   Harrison Valley, Pa.

The fact that few people know well this quiet little fellow is no reason that he is not known by all of us. He used to teach school and one day he realized there were a lot more things he wanted to know. His experience in the field have given him a more serious outlook, but his quiet manner and interest in his work win the friendship of his fellows.

29

EDWARD DORSETT   Mansfield, Pa.
                "EDDY"

Y. M. C. A.; Intramural Basketball.

This renowned lad is no less than a humanly animated encyclopedia of English, French and German. How so much knowledge can find place in one small head has puzzled Mansfield philosophers for years.

"Eddy" is one of the finest chaps going. His winning personality and notworthy achievements are destined to carry him far. Mansfield is proud to graduate a person of such high standing.

WILLARD EHLERS   Horseheads, N. Y.
                "DUTCH"

Willard is said to have the best bass voice at Mansfield State. Anyone who has heard him in the "Four Horsemen" and his other various roles will testify as to his ability. When he blows his big bass sax the whole campus shakes and we might call him the base on which the school stands.

JAIRUS GAVITT   Sonestown, Pa.
                "JERRY"

"M" Club; Varsity Football (1) (2) (3) (4); Flashlight Staff (1) (2); Emersonian Literary Society; Y. M. C. A.

Hail, Hail to "Jerry" political haranguer supreme! We expect him to win a Tammany Hall of his own some day. And why not? He is a strenuous worker and has engaged in many activities while at Mansfield. Football and practical jokes have occupied a part of his time—not to forget that he was one of the original Flashlight Editors.

CARLTON HARKNESS   Mansfield, Pa.
                "DOC"

Y. M. C. A.; Varsity Football (1) (2) (3) (4);
Senior Programs (4); *Member Comets, Basketball
Champs* (2).

Hannibal had an easier time getting his army
across the Alps than we have in attempting to show
our keen appreciation of having "Doc" for a friend,
a pal and ally. But after all why try to inscribe
something of which "Doc" is already aware. If you
are a friend of his, the biggest tribute lies in the
fact that he recognizes you as such. Four years ago
a few of us started as trembling greenies, suspicious
of each other. Now "Doc" is leaving with a friendship only death can break.

HENRY HILFIGER   Ulysses, Pa.

Y. M. C. A.

Henry is one of the more mature members of
our class, who takes studying rather seriously. He
was a high school principal for three years, but decided to come to Mansfield to get one of the coveted
sheep-skins. Although he will not graduate until
August, we are proud to call him one of the class of
1929.

EDWARD HILL   Wellsboro, Pa.

Varsity Baseball (1) (2) (3) (4); *Varsity
Football* (1) (2) (3) (4).

The round peg in the round hole, that's "Eddie."
He earned an enviable reputation for himself here in
both football and baseball. He is also an enthusiastic
pursuer of happiness. Any suggestion that promises
a good time has his whole support, and once accep-
ted, nobody enjoys himself more than "Eddie." Mansfield will miss him.

31

MARY HANNAH HOWE   Mansfield, Pa.
"SUNNY"

Secretary and Treasurer, Dramatic Club; Rurban Club.

We call her "Sunny." When you're discouraged just tune in on M. H. H. Talented? Oh, yes! Have you read her little book of poems? Have you heard her sing? Did you see her as the heroine in the "Boomerang"?

Those of us who know her best claim her to be one of the finest. "She opens in each heart a little heaven."

RUTH L. HUTHMAKER   Wyoming, Pa.

Domicilian Club; Art Club; Glee Club; Y. W. C. A.; Outdoor Club; Carontawan Board (4).

"Oh, the world is wide, and the world is grand,
    And there's little or nothing new.
But the sweetest thing is the grip of the hand
    Of the friend that's tried and true."

KENTLEY R. JONES, JR.   Wyoming, Pa.

Emersonian Literary Society (1) (2) (3); Treasurer (4); Carontawan Board (1); Y. M. C. A. (1) (2); Cabinet (3) (4); Glee Club (1) (2) (3); Student Council (1); Flashlight Staff (1); Class Secretary (2) ;"Y" Minstrels (1); Debating Team (4).

Pausing to prognosticate we expect to see Kentley occupying a supreme court chair or a similar high position. Kentley waxes strong in argument and we predict he will make an able lawyer.

No matter what joy befalls him, we shall remember him as the fellow who kept sleepy classes wide awake with "wise-cracks" and timely questions.

FRANCIS KELLY   Lambs Creek, Pa.
                    'KELL''

Varsity Baseball, Basketball (1) (2) (3) (4);
Varsity Football (2) (3); Vice President Senior
Class (4).

A man as superb in his ideal as he is in
physique. When you know a person for four years
there is no half way mark. He either measures to
a high peak or ebbs to insignificance, and "Kell"
has never once dropped from the pedestal on which
we placed him during our first year. If he performs
in life as he did on the court, gridiron and diamond
he will make the records of post-college life crash as
dizzily as he did Mansfield's.

MARGARET KREBS   Keating Summit, Pa.
                    "KREBIE"

Y. W. C. A.

Krebie reminds us of that well-known little girl
—the one who had the equally well-known curl
somewhere about the middle of the front portion of
her forehead. The stage lost a fine comedienne when
it lost "Krebie", but we gained a real friend.

MYRLE LEE   Carbondale, Pa.

Emersonian Literary Society; President, Dramatic Club; Rurban Club.

Here is one who can laugh in spite of everything. In clever vaudeville skits, in coaching a play,
in being a health clown, Myrle is fine, for he possesses much dramatic ability. Hats off! Here comes
the Dramatic Club President, a president who has
made the Dramatic Club a successful organization.

33

GUIDA E. MARROW   Trucksville, Pa.

Emersonian Literary Society (1) (2); *Rurban Club* (2) (4); *Play* (2); *Dramatic Club* (1) (2); *Y. W. C. A. Cabinet* (2) (3); *Treasurer of Class* (2); *Flashlight Staff* (2) (3); *Student Council* (3); *Carontawan Board* (4).

If there is any activity that Guida hasn't had a part in, let it speak now or forever hold its peace. No situation has yet been known to down that infallible source of dry caustic wit for which she is noted. Guida can expound in long harangues on her philosophy of life. Many intense moments of literary effort has she spent that Mansfield Seniors might grace the pages of history.

AGNES McCAUSLAND   Mansfield, Pa.
"AG"

Emersonian Literary Society (3) (4); *Rurban Club* (3); *Play* (3); *Secretary* (4); *Dramatc Club* (1) (2); *Glee Club* (1) (2) (3); *Y. W. C. A.; Vice President Junior Class* (3); *Flashlight Staff* (2) (3); *Carontawan Board* (4).

Priceless prop of the Carontawan Board! It would take another "Ag" to write up this dispenser of wit and talent. How she ever finds time between social activities and teaching to push the literary pen, is still a mystery, but were it not for her divine inspiration, a large number of the class would have gone "write-up-less". "Ag" is a devotee of the dreaded French courses and rakes in A's with a calmness that amazes us all.

HELEN H. MEAGLEY   Hallstead, Pa.
"HELEN LOUISE"

Art Club; Rurban Club; Y. W. C. A.

"Helen Louise'" may seem reserved to all those not acquainted with her, but beneath her quiet and loving manner she is always ready for a good time. Perhaps in her Senior year few recognize her name. Why? She became tired of being a Miss and is now a fond Mrs.

PAUL R. MILLER   Mansfield, Pa.
"PEORY"

Varsity Basketball (1) (2) (3) (4); Captain
'28; Carontawan Editor (4); Dramatic Club (1);
President (2).

"Peory" is the nearest thing to Abe Lincoln in
the college, the only difference is that Abe freed
slaves and Paul makes slaves. He has enslaved
everybody's friendship from Lambs Creek to Holcomb Center. For some reason he's very intellectual,
high in literary ability and exceedingly good as an
athlete. You need not look beneath the surface to
find a man. It sticks out all over. Our votes for
"Joe Popularity" go to Paul.

HENRY OBELKEVITCH   Throop, Pa.
"OBIE"

"M" Club (3); Football (1) (2) (3) (4); Captain (4); Y. M. C. A.; Magician.

Many famous men have come from Throop—
among them "Hank" Obelkevitch, the captain of our
fighting football team. He has been one of the big
men in college during the past four years. He is one
of the great players who has worn the Red and
Black and has done his share in warding off would-
be invaders of Mansfield's goal line.

Hank's easy manner and generous smile should
help him make and keep many friends wherever he
goes.

GEORGE PALMER   Mansfield, Pa.
"PETE"

Orchestra (1) (2) (3) (4); Music Supervisors'
Club; Glee Club; Opera.

A cheery, happy pal is George, always looking
for a good time and usually finding it. He is leader
of the "Red and Blacks" which is bringing happiness to the countryside and school.

George is, in music and personality, a favorite.
There is no instrument that he cannot play.

AGNES M. PERSONS   Susquehanna, Pa.
                    "PAT"

Domicilian Club; Y. W. C. A.; Art Club; Hiking Club; Junior High School Quarterly Board; Flashlight Board.

"A friend is a present we give ourselves."
That's one of our old time songs.
So we put "Pat" down with the best of them
For that's where she belongs.
Among the friends we have given ourselves
Most comforting, tried and true
The one that we oftenest think about,
Is the gift to ourselves of you.

FRANCES L. PHILP   Edinboro, Pa.
                    "FRAN"

Domicilian Club; Y. W. C. A.; Emersonian Literary Society; President W. S. G. A .

"The best friend we have is the one who endeavors to be his best self for our sake, and to provoke us to our best. This is a higher, harder task than that of surrendering one's own will for a friend's sake."

WILFORD C. POMEROY   Roulette, Pa.
                    "POMIE"

Y. M. C. A.

"Pomie" entered here the second semester, coming to us from Lock Haven Teachers College. While there he played varsity football for three years, and had a fine record as a student, which he has ably carried on here. He has a fine personality and has been a ready co-operator in school activities during his short stay with us.

FRED RINGROSE   Berwick, Pa.

President of Supervisors' Club (26) (29); *"Y"*
Minstrels (2) (3) (4); *Band* (2) (3) (4); *Red and*
Blacks; Y. M. C. A.; Male Quartet (3); *Chorus.*

"Fritz" is among the best pianists and composers of the school. He holds down the percussion
section of both band and orchestra, and so far we
have not found his equal in this work.

"Fritz" will always be known to us as a jolly
fellow with a smile for everybody, and one who has
made a mark in the world.

ELEANORE RUMSEY   Mansfield, Pa.

Student Council (3).

First Degree Student: "Among the students of
Mansfield, there is one that stands out. That is
Eleanore."

Second Degree Student: "You're right. What is
there about her that makes everyone like her? She
isn't always shouting here and there to make herself conspicuous and popular. How is it that everyone has a good word for her?"

First Student: "She's just her natural self."

EVELYN SCHMOLL   Kingston, Pa.

'ABIE'

Outdoor Club, President (4); *Y. W. C. A.;*
Hiking Club; Dramatic Club (1).

Underneath her carefree, fun-loving nature,
she is serious and is a girl who desires the best of
life and gives her best in return. "Abie" is a good
student, but often finds time to read letters from a
"frank" young man.

ARDEN SEELY   Mansfield, Pa.

Arden's ambitions, which are many and varied, are backed by a purpose that will prove their realization. We are not certain from whom he inherited his capacity for hard work, but are certain that he possesses it.

Whenever we come to Mansfield we'll expect to see Arden around somewhere, the same as ever.

HUGH SEELYE   Mansfield, Pa.

Hugh is another one of those pleasant fellows whom you simply like. Instead of dancing to love, Hugh loves to dance—his are among the nimblest feet on the floor. Hugh may be said to be quiet, that is, until one knows him well. This reserve stands him in good stead. Remember that all truly great men are dignified and reserved.

ANTHONY SHELINSKI   Dickson City, Pa.
              "TONY"

Football (1) (2); Glee Club (1) (2); President Rurban Club (3); Business Manager Flashlight (3); Dramatic Club (1) (2) (3) (4); Treasurer (3); Vice President (4); Business Manager Carontawan (4); Visual Aids (1) (2) (3) (4); Men's Council (4).

We all figure that Tony has a controlling interest in the institution because he has been business manager of nearly everything in the College but the Domicilian Club and the Girls' Hiking Club. "Tony" is a member of the Student Council, but in spite of that fact he is popular. What more can be said of any man?

38

BOGHDAN SHLANTA

Supervisors' Club; Orchestra (1) (2) (3) (4); *Glee Club; Band* (1) (2); *String Quartet.*

Boghdan is known as a rising young man who has given many concerts and recitals over the radio. The school has enjoyed his playing on the violin and on the 'cello, which he plays in the orchestra. We may well be proud of him.

IVA SNYDER   Waymart, Pa.
          "IVE"

Y. W. C. A.; Das Vereinlein; Athletic Club (1).

Another follower of Aristotle! "Give me the real things of life," says Iva, "but prove it first by Science." Iva is a very conscientious student and while gazing into the crystal, she has made plans to be a very efficient school teacher, who will, in the near future, obtain her Master and Doctor Degrees.

LA RUE M. STANTON   Mansfield, Pa.
          "RUE

Y. M. C. A. (1) (2) (3) (4).

Here is an excellent mathematician! As to co-operation and cheerfulness "Rue" is above reproach. He is an asset to the recreational life of the school in dancing, hiking, tennis, and baseball. Altogether Stanton is a true friend.

39

WARREN STEELE   Mansfield, Pa.

Rurban Club; Y. M. C. A.

This year we woke up to the fact that we had been missing one of the finest men in the class because of his quietness. While another man is still talking, Warren has gone ahead and done whatever is necessary, and done it just a little better than most of us would do it. He possesses what psychologists call a "keen analytical mind"; which is capable of grasping whatever problem confronts it.

LLOYD STRAUGHN   Mansfield, Pa.

Football (1) (2) (3) (4); *Basketball* (2) (3) (4); *Dramatic Club; Carontawan* (4).

An epitome of Lloyd's stay at college would disclose that he is one of the campus' leaders. His six feet of immenseness overshadow all gloom. Thus he never lets life worry him as long as his grades are in black ink.

A very promising future lies ahead of "Doc". Advantages of higher education in American and foreign universities, combined with native talent, and a commanding presence, will make Lloyd one of the big men of future decades.

LURAY SWARTZ   Hughesville, Pa.

Luray's assured air informed us that he was a person worthy of our notice. He came here with a well defined purpose in mind and lived through the years to boast that he had achieved his aim. More mature than the usual run of college students, he did not mix to a large extent with the students. His studies were his friends. We cannot but admire a conscientious fellow of his type.

DOROTHY L. THOMAS   Hazleton, Pa.
"DOT"

Domicilian Club; Y. W. C. A.; Art Club; Hiking Club.

"From the day when first we start,
Each in life to play his part,
'Til we reach that perfect peace
Where all trial and care shall cease,
Fate can nothing better send than
A true and loyal friend."

WALTER URBAN   Liberty, Pa.

Rurban Club.

Walt's fame rests upon his ability for hard work, mental or physical. Walt is also a lover of the wide open spaces. Many a night he has slumbered on the hillside back of the college. Farewell, Walt, to you and your flivver.

FRANCES WALDRCN   Washington, D. C.
"FRAN"

Emersonian Literary Society; Athletic Club; Y. W. C. A.; Hiking Club; Art Club.

"Somebody said it couldn't be done,
But "Fran", with a smile, replied,
That maybe it couldn't, but she would be one
Who wouldn't say no 'til she tried.
So she knuckled right in with her face set and grim,
If she worried, she hid it by smiling;
She started to sing as she tackled the thing
That couldn't be done, and she did it."

41

BERNICE WEBSTER   Tioga, Pa.

" 'Tis not my wish to labor long for fame,
Then sip her wine;
This task is mine—
To send my Soul out greater than it came."

FRANK YURKEWITCH   Elkland, Pa.

"YURKIE"

Band (1) (2) (3) (4); Orchestra (1) (2) (3)
(4); Glee Club; President Supervisors' Club '28;
"Y" Minstrels (2) (3); Y. M. C. A. Gospel Team
(2) (3); Carontawan Board (4).

Frank is a bassoon player of no mean calibre
in the band and orchestra, a promising student-
composer of the school with a deliberate but firm
mind. He is ready and willing to help at any time,
always the same, a capable, dependable fellow,
bound for a real future.

Seniors

Groups I and II

RACHAEL ADAMS   Roulette, Pa.
'RAE'"

Art Club; Y. W. C. A.

Tall, fair-haired and blue-eyed is our sweet dispositioned "Rae". When "Rae" makes a friend she keeps one, but no wonder she doesn't bother with the men of Mansfield—Alfred University means too much for anything here. Well, "Rae", although Lock Haven was your Alma Mater once, we hope Mansfield will be the more lasting of the two.

ELLA ATEN   Factoryville, Pa.
"TRUDY"

Hiking Club (1) (2); *Y. W. C. A.* (1) (2); *Athletic Club* (1) (2).

"Much in little"—that's Ella. She's just our idea of a girl, cheerful, sincere and ambitious. She's a fourth floor booster who is always ready for mirthful activities. Nightly feeds have winked at her and said, "You'll miss me, sister, when you're dead."

EDDIE AUGUSTINE   Alden, Pa.
"EDDIE"

Varsity Baseball '28; Basketball '28; Assistant Art Editor, Carontawan '29.

Meet our artist friend from the coal fields. That's where Eddie got his start. Every fence post in the Alden coal yards tells where Eddie spent his summer. No, he wasn't just amusing the employees drawing pictures; he was keeping in trim for his job as assistant art editor.

FANNY AUSTIN   Roaring Branch, Pa.
                  "FAN"
Y. W. C. A.

"True-hearted, whole-hearted,
Faithful and loyal."

It's always a friendly greeting and an agreeable
countenance that we meet when we encounter "Fan"
in the corridor. The faithfulness of "Fan" and
Lysle will not soon be forgotten by us fellow classmates.

LOIS E. AYERS   Old Forge, Pa.
                  "LOVEY"
Athletic Club; Hockey (1) (2).

Lois is one of the "Beach Nuts". She is always
happy and smiling, is great at hockey and a whiz at
playing the ukelele. We are sure the annex will
miss her next year.
She has an unlimited amount of energy and pep
and is always ready to join in anything to have a
good time.

NELLIE BAER   Shickshinny, Pa.
                  "CUBBY"
Y. W. C. A. (1) (2); Outdoor Club (1).

"Should old acquaintance be forgot and never
brought to mind?" Should they? Well not if they
are like Nellie. Nellie doesn't believe they should
either. Just to prove it, steal into her room some
day and catch her with that far away look in her
eyes. I wonder whom she is dreaming about. Well,
that's for her to tell.

HARRIET BAKER   Troy, Pa.

A lover of instruction is always well instructed. Harriet is known for her high marks in class. She is peppy, full of fun and always a worth while friend.

BLISS BANKER   Ansonia, Pa.

Ansonia is famous for countless wonders—but the greatest of these is Bliss. His sincerity, his conviviality, his genial smile have made him a welcome figure about the campus. Bliss was a member of the January graduating group.

ALICE BARKER   Ulysses, Pa.
Y. W. C. A.

Never is Alice more pleased than when she is helping someone and scattering sunshine, brightening the corner where she is. Never has she been known to get cranky. Her uniformly even "unruffle-able" disposition has won for her many a staunch and loyal friend.

ELLEN BAXTER   West Franklin, Pa.

"Still as a mouse." But when you see her eyes twinkle and the corners of her mouth turn up as that characteristic droll remark slips out, you just know something's happened and you know who did it, too!

She does forget to attend class occasionally, but she never forgets her friends.

HAZELLE BEATTIE   Pittsburgh, Pa.
              "PETE"

Y. W. C. A.

"Pete" has been with us only one year, but in that time we have found out some of her charming qualities. Athletics seem to be her chief hobby— especially basketball. We're sorry we couldn't see more of you, "Pete".

OLGA BELT   Mansfield, Pa.

"The love of learning, the sequestered nooks,
And all the sweet serenity of books."

Here is one who has an unusual share of ability in all the arts. Her sincere straight-forwardness makes Olga one of the truest members of 1929.

NORMA BENDER   Susquehanna, Pa.

"NORM"

Yes, this is Norma! To look at her, one would think that she is always quiet and studious. First impressions are usually lasting, but here is an exception to the rule. Whenever a good time is at hand, Norma is at hand, too. As a teacher she will make a success for she possesses those qualities which a teacher needs.

MAJORIE E. BERLEW   Factoryville, Pa.

"MARJ"

Y. W. C. A. (1) (2); At*hletic Club* (1) (2); *Hockey* (1).

"Marj" is the kind of a girl people don't forget. Spend five minutes in the presence of this charming maiden and your troubles, worries, and cares will go up in smoke.

"Marj's" interests range from athletics to literature. She certainly is successful as a guard on the basketball court and she wields a mean hockey sitck.

HELEN BRADFORD   Troy, Pa.

"Smile and the world smiles with you," seems to be Helen's motto. She is thoroughly liked by everyone because of her earnestness, sincerity and ability. Helen has proved herself a genius through her work in the Model School. We are sure she will be a successful and efficient teacher.

NETTA LOU BRENNEMAN   Factoryville, Pa.

"NETTA LOU"

Y. W. C. A. (1) (2); *Cecelian Glee Club* (1);
Art Club (1) (2).

Lovable, laughable and adorable are a few of
the adjectives we may use in describing Netta Lou.
She has a bewitchingly different personality. Anita
Loos must have been referring to her when she
wrote "Gentlemen Prefer Blonds."

AGNES BROWN   Middletown, N. Y.

Athletic Club; Y. W. C. A.

"Somewhere a voice is calling"—(down the register chute)—"*Come* on Bud. It's time for breakfast."

But we're forced to forgive Agnes for even
that, because we love her. 'Tis reported that her
smile brings to earth even such deities as college
football coaches and captains. Success? Nonsense!
She's bound to have it.

HELEN BROWN   Wyalusing, Pa.

Y. W. C. A.; Hiking Club.

Oh, what a common name! Yes, it may be common, but it isn't a common person who owns this
name. When it comes to eating and fun we can
always count on Helen. But, Helen means business
when she gets serious and settles down to study.

MILDRED BROWN   Ulster, Pa.

Y. W. C. A.; Outdoor Club; Athletic Club.

Blue eyes, light hair, a perfect blonde and a worth while companion. She is vivacious and full of fun. Mildred is studious as is shown by her high scholastic record. She is outstanding as a hockey, basketball and baseball player.

BEULAH BRYANT   Honesdale, Pa.

Y. W. C. A.; Athletic Club.

"If you can hear the whispering about you
And never yield or deal in whispers, too;
If you can bravely smile when loved ones
        doubt you
And never doubt in turn what loved ones do;
If you can keep a sweet and gentle spirit
In spite of fame or fortune, rank or place,
And though you win your goal or only near it
Can win with poise or lose with equal grace"—
We're quite sure McEvoy must have had a girl like Beulah in mind when he wrote this.

MARION BURT   Coudersport, Pa.

Y. W. C. A.

Marion is one of our down town students. She is studious, quiet and well-liked by all who know her. Her one great outlook on life is school-teaching. We know she will make a great success at this by her winning smile. It makes life more worth while to know people like Marion, and her hosts of friends sincerely wish her the best of everything in life.

50

MONETA BUSH   Westfield, Pa.
                "NETA"
Y. W. C. A.; Athletic Club.

"There is no treasure which may be compared unto
    a faithful friend;
Gold soon decayeth and wordly wealth consumeth,
    and wasteth in the wind;
But friendship once planted in a perfect and pure
    mind endureth weal and woe."

VERNETTE L. BUTTS   Plains, Pa.

Y. W. C. A.; Athletic Club.

A cure for the blues is vivacious Vernette with
her ever present wit and understanding sympathy.
She must be the own child of old man "Wit and
Humor". Can't you see her eyes just sparkle with
fun and mischief?

ESTHER CAMPBELL   Athens, Pa.

Y. W. C. A.; Outdoor Club.

She is faithful to her studies and her friends
and is always present when you need her most. With
these qualities we see no reason why her teaching
career should not be a decided success.

LEAH CASS   Nelson, Pa.

Outdoor Club; Y. W. C. A.

Leah is the proud possessor of the most contagious laugh in North Hall. At first glance she gives the impression of being shy and reserved, but those who know her say that she is always ready for fun.

KATHLEEN COLLINS   Susquehanna, Pa.

One look at her picture unmistakably guarantees that she will succeed in life with the same alertness and capability that has characterized her thus far.

GERTRUDE COOK   Dushore, Pa.

"For it stirs the blood in a person's heart
And makes his pulses fly,
To catch the thrill of her happy voice,
And the light of her pleasant eye."

MABEL COOTS   Canisteo, N. Y.

Here's another superior student known by the
teachers as well as the students. She is very interested in dentistry.

"What! sigh for the toothache? No, there was
never yet a philosopher that could endure the toothache patiently."

LEONA MARIE CORSON   New Albany, Pa.

"NONIE"

Y. W. C. A.; Student Council, Summer '28; Secretary Rurban Club '28.

She seems a quiet maiden but appearances are
often deceiving. She never allows her good times
to interfere with her work, for she devotes a great
deal of time to her lessons. Because of her willingness to work and her fine abilities, we know she will
succeed.

HELEN CREDIFORD   Waterville, Pa.

Y. W. C. A. (2); Hiking Club (2).

"She's full of life, she's full of fun,
'Twould be hard to find a better one."

She's intent, unobtrusive, and usually serious.
Because of her personality she has played a leading
part in our friendship and is worthy of true success.

53

IONA DAVIES   Kingston, Pa.
                "IONE"

Art Club (2); Vice President (1); Y. W. C. A. (1).

Iona is another of our lovable prospective teachers. She is a hard worker, which accounts for her high standing in teaching. She is good to look upon, good to hear, and good to think on. A sweeter disposition and a more amiable personality you will have to look long to find.

BEATRICE DAVIS   Kingsley, Pa.
                "BEATY"

This blue-eyed maiden is one we all adore. Her ambition in life involves two things: first, to make a success in teaching, then to lose the dimple in her chin.

MARGUERITE DAVIS   Middlebury Center, Pa.
                "PEG"

Y. W. C. A. Cabinet; Emersonian Society; Hiking Club; Athletic Club; Y. W. C. A.

When "Peg" says she will do a thing you can depend upon her doing it. She has opinions of her own and is not afraid to express them. "Peg" has a well developed sense of humor and, this, added to a kind heart, has gained for her a wide circle of friends.

MARY JANE DAVISON   Canton, Pa.

Mary is a musician by nature, a good student, and everybody's friend. True to her name, she is always merry and knows how to make others merry, too. We wish her success and happiness.

KATHERINE DEWEY   Harrisburg, Pa.
                "KAY"

Glee Club; Y. W. C. A.

It is difficult to say how much people's minds are conciliated by a kind manner and a pleasing way. "Kay" is always sowing seeds of kindness wherever she goes. She will be sure to win in this world.

BLANCHE DOTY   Sabinsville, Pa.

Art Club; Y. W. C. A.

Blanche has a subtle wit, and a heart as warm as they make them. She is the original conundrum to everyone who doesn't know her and to some of us who do. There's a "great big reason" (in Westfield) why there aren't any men around here.

DORIS EDWARDS   Susquehanna, Pa.

"ED"

Y. W. C. A.

Always hurried, never flurried, always good-natured and ready for anything anywhere, anytime —that's Doris. There has to be a girl like her in every class or it would not be a class. When Doris teaches school there's one thing her pupils will be sure to get and that's a musical training.

FRANCES EGAN   Scranton, Pa.

Y. W. C. A.; Athletic Club; Secretary (2).

Just a sweet Irish Rose
But about the nicest kind that grows.
Sparkling, laughing, mischievous brown eyes,
That leave in their wake faint-hearted masculine
    sighs.
The kind of a teacher a child will adore,
All of this, of whom could we ask more?

RUTH EISLE   Scranton, Pa.

Y. W. C. A. (1); *Cabinet* (2); *Athletic Club* (1); *Treasurer* (2).

The face that sank a thousand ships—well, maybe not that many, but she has sunk a lot of hopes held by the stronger sex. Ruth has more than a pretty face. She was adored by her pupils, liked by her teachers, admired and loved by classmates.

HAZEL ELVIDGE · Throop, Pa.
"RED"

Athletic Club; Hockey Team.

Mystery lurks in those grey-green eyes and such charm is revealed in that sudden smile—Hazel, who knows all the latest dance steps and uses the newest catch-words so flippantly!

Secret—"Red's" favorite pastime is collecting letters from members of visiting teams.

SUSIE ENGLISH Coudersport, Pa.

Y. W. C. A.

Surely you all know Susie with her sparkling eyes and ever-ready fun. After you have met her you will remember her. Is she popular? Ask the poor mail man who has to deliver her daily dozen of letters. Carefree, gay, studious, and friendly is Susie.

ADRIAN FISK Wyalusing, Pa.

This is my creed: "To do some good, to bear my ills without complaining; to strive to be when each day dies some better than the morning found me; to keep my standards always high; to find my task and always do it."

JULIA FOLEY   Nanticoke, Pa.
"JUDY"

Yes, she has brown eyes, the kind of eyes that see things. Underneath that comfortably calm exterior lies a great deal of mischief. Perseverance is her greatest asset and we well believe she will always win as great success in future life as she has at M. S. T. C.

ESTHER FOWLER   Galeton, Pa.

Esther is an individual whose "self" radiates sunshine. If you need help, she's right on the job. We're sure she'll succeed in the teaching profession.

ELIZABETH FOX   Wyalusing, Pa.

We predict a "Vini-Vidi-Vinci" future for this charter member of the Smith House. She has proved herself highly capable in both professional and academic subjects during the time she has been with us. In addition to being a star student, she can also enjoy fun, and lots of it.

SARAH FRANCIS   Wyoming, Pa.

Y. W. C. A.

This modest maiden is charming and quiet with
a dignified manner and winning ways. She always
seems happy and busy about something. We do not
know what her ambition is, yet we are assured her
quiet nature will find its niche in the world. A good
friend and pal—we are glad to have had this miss
in our class.

CELIA E. FRANK   Meshoppen, Pa.

"FRANKY"

Art Club; Y. W. C. A.; Emersonian Literary
Society; Athletic Club; Hockey.

"A merry heart maketh a cheerful countenance."

Since Celia can't leave herself here, we wish
she would leave us her contagious smile and friendly
greetings. But we know Celia will want to charm
others as she has charmed us. She has been known
all through her college career for her good work in
class, her ready loyalty to M. S. T. C., and that
crowning gift, her friendly personality.

ETHEL FROST   Moosic, Pa.

"PROSTIE"

Cecelian Glee Club; Athletic Club; Y. W. C. A.;
Hiking Club; Tribunal; Hockey; Baseball; Basketball.

"Give me a basketball and content will I be."
A good captain? Well rather!
A good sport? None better!
Can she play hockey? Well, yes!
We have liked Ethel because she has been frank,
unaffected, and just brimming over with pep. She
is a friend we won't forget. Speaking of student
teachers—step aside—here comes Ethel.

ARLENE GOODRIDGE   Genesee, Pa.

"GOODRIDGE"

Y. W. C. A. (1); *Art Club* (1).

Tall and debonair, combined with good looks and a sweet disposition make her lovable to all. Her sly humor generally comes with such a surprise that it evokes laughter from all present.

Arlene believes in the old maxim reversed, "Do not do today what you can put off till tomorrow." But you should see her work the night before a Primary Reading unit is due.

ADA E. GRANDONI   Old Forge Pa.

"ADIE"

Athletic Club; Y. W. C. A.; Hockey.

"Whatsoever it is, be it work or play,
It is well done in Ada's way."

It is the gift of art, combined with expressive brown eyes, sparkling with fun, playing "hide and seek," that makes Ada one of our class favorites. She is the kind of a girl whose personality shines forth in every act. Her many friends acclaim her as a willing worker and a steadfast friend.

HELEN GRIFFIN   Kingston, Pa.

Athletic Club; Hiking Club; Y. W. C. A.; Outdoor Club; Athletic Club Minstrels.

A blond whirlwind, typifying jubilant enthusiasm, burts in upon our calm and philosophical reveries. She throws herself on our carefully made beds and says something like this: "Say, kids, that was a great dance. Listen, let me tell you, I've met a new man."

60

HELEN E. HAIGHT   Canton, Pa.

  Athletic Club; Emersonian Literary Society
(2); Y. W. C. A.; Student Council (2).

"Whatever the weather may be," says she,
"Whatever the weather may be,
It's the songs ye sing, and the smiles ye wear
That's a-making the sunshine everywhere."

BLANCHE HARER   Covington, Pa.
               "DUTCHY"

  "I love the play of every day,
  And all the life force that we see;
  To build anew and carry through
  And just to live is joy to me."

AMANDA NAOMI HARRIS   Pittston, Pa.
            "NYM"

  *Emersonian Society; Athletic Club; Y. W. C.
A.; Outdoor Club.*

  At any time when one hears laughter and fun,
"Nym" is sure to be present adding her bit. You
can usually hear members of both sexes inquiring
where Harris is or what she is doing.

PERYLE HECK   Tioga, Pa.

Y. W. C. A.; Hiking Club.

"The force of her own merit makes her way."
We know very little of Peryle because she finds
Tioga life more interesting. What we do know of
her is of the best and highest quality. We know that
luck and success will not pass her by.

MARGARET HENDRYX   Coudersport, Pa.
                    "PEG"

Glee Club (1).

"As modest and sweet as ever a maid could be."

Margaret believes in helping others. If you
ever want help go to "Peg". You'll probably find
her engaged in reading a book.

CHRISTINE HENRY   Ulysses, Pa.
                   "CHRISTIE"

Y. W. C. A.

Christine has proved a true friend to all who
know her, and is as good a student as she is a pal.
She undertakes any task which is assigned her, and
sees it through. She enjoys her week-ends at home,
but when she remains here her mail box is closely
guarded.

MARION HICKOX   Gibson, Pa.

Y. W. C. A.

Marian came to us this year after having
taught for a season. Because of the fact that she
lives down town and is quiet and studious by nature,
we do not know too much about her. Those who are
associated with her in school work find that her
experience in teaching is a great advantage to her
and to them. She plans to continue in the work now
that she has graduated from Mansfield.

VIRGINIA ELIZABETH HICKS   Mill City, Pa.

"JINNY"

Y. W. C. A.; Hiking Club.

This is "Jinny's" first year in the dorm and she
surely has added much gaiety to second floor.
Her brown eyes and beautiful black hair certainly make South Hall, as well as North Hall, sit
up and take notice. Wherever we find "Jinny" we
find fun.

ELEANORE HILBORN   Cedar Run, Pa.

"HIBBY"

Y. W. C. A. (2); Hiking Club (2).

This favored daughter of Aphrodite is often
solemnly angelic in appearance, but she has a never-
failing supply of jokes. "Hibby" likes good times
and is always around when refreshments are men-
tioned. After all she is painstaking and persistent.
If she does worry a little perhaps, that is what
makes the result satisfactory.

MARGARET HOLLAND   Liberty, Pa.
                "JIGGS"
Y. W. C. A.

" 'Tis good to be merry and wise,
'Tis good to be honest and true."

We are happy to say that "Jiggs" lives up to
these virtues. "Merry" seems to be her middle name,
for she keeps the "Brace Brigade" howling most of
the time.

We know that she will be a splendid teacher.
Good luck, "Jiggs"!

HELEN HOWARD   Painted Post, N. Y.
                "PETIE"

Athletic Club; Student Council (2); Dramatic
Club.

This winsome face does not seek attention, but
cannot fail to attract it. "Petie" is a rare compound
of duty, frolic, and fun. When life becomes bore-
some, and entertainment is lacking, Helen always
has an idea of some stirring activity to offer.

MIRIAM HOWELLS   Olyphant, Pa.

Athletic Club (1) (2); Y. W. C. A.; Dramatic
Club (2); Glee Club (1); Student Council (1) (2).

You'll hear her laugh; you'll see her smile,
you'll put her down with the best of them, because
that's where "Our Bud" belongs.

She specializes in most anything during class
hours, but she's making a special study of a well-
known school editor during other hours.

Her aim?   Grand Opera—see you at the
Metropolitan, "Buddie."

64

MICHAEL HRYCENKO   Breslau, Pa.

Varsity Football (2) (3); *"M" Club.*

A deep bass voice, a good clean countenance, a good pal, a strong personality, and that's "Mike."

This good athlete came to us with the name of "The Hanover Flash!" He may well be called the "Mansfield Flash" for the work he's done for us in football and basketball.

GENEVIEVE HUNTINGTON   Canisteo, N. Y.

We need more girls like Gertrude. She is as steady as a rock, dependable, lovable, and in short a lot of "-ables" combined. She is a loyal defender of Mansfield and thinks that college life is certainly grand.

GENEVIEVE INGLEY   Shinglehouse, Pa.
          ' GEN'

Art Club; Glee Club; Y. W. C. A.

One look at Genevieve is enough to make us feel the strength of her personality. Some say that she is very quiet and dignified, but her loyal friends fail to see it, for back of those jolly eyes lurks a spirit of innocent mischief. Her career will be a successful one.

MARGARET INMAN   Wellsburg, N. Y.
"MEG"

Hiking Club (1); *Art Club* (1).

M is for merriment
E is for enthusiasm
G is for graciousness
One of the happy girls of 'The Down Town Gang." She has blue eyes and a merry laugh. We are glad that we can have her with us for she signifies what her name really means—a pearl.

LYSLE IRVING   Ogdensburg, Pa.

Y. W. C. A.

"When night hath set her silver lamps on high,
Then is the time for study."

Do you know Lysle, the most studious girl in North Hall? This isn't hyperbole, just plain truth.

Lysle's one of those quiet girls, but when one knows her she just radiates sunshine with her smile, and bubbles over with fun.

RACHEL JANICELLI   Forest City, Pa.
"RAY"

Cecelian Glee Club; Y. W. C. A.; Outdoor Club.

"A friend in need is a friend indeed."

Rachel is one of those persons you just turn to in trouble. They say she is reserved and aloof, but those who are fortunate enough to know her recognize her true worth. She certainly doesn't lack ambition in her studies as any of the teachers will tell you.

DORA JELLIFF   Covington, Pa.
        "RED"

She's what we call a friend.
    "One whose grip is a little tighter,
    One whose smile is a little brighter,
    One who is the same today as tomorrow,
    One who will share your joy and sorrow."
That's why she's our friend.

JULIA JOHNSON   Wellsboro, Pa.

    Although Julia Johnson sounds like a movie
queen, Julia's Hollywood is Mansfield. We know she
could act in wild-western pictures, especially in
vitaphone productions with that voice of hers. She
surely can tell exciting stories about the great open
spaces of Wellsboro.

ELEANORE JONES   Taylor, Pa.

    Rurban Club; Athletic Club.

    Eleanore isn't the athletic type, nor is she a
quiet little girl; but then how could she be and belong · to the "Taylor Gang," too? Really we think
she's the magazine cover type and that's not all of
it either. Eleanore is popular at the dance and is
never at loss for a partner.

67

KATHLEEN JOYCE   Wilkes-Barre, Pa.

"KAY"

Hiking Club; Y. W. C. A.; Athletic Club; Glee Club; Tribunal.

She is made to engage all hearts and charm all eyes. She is good without pretense and is blessed with plain reason and sober sense. "Kay" is unaffected and composed in mind.

MARTHA JUNE   Shickshinny, Pa.

"JUNE"

Y. W. C. A.; Art Club; Outdoor Club.

Martha knows that everything a student-teacher does, whether good or poor, counts either for or against her rating. But that isn't what we want to remember about her. What we want to find out is on whom she has her heart set: the boy friend at Muhlenburg, the one at State College, or the one at Oglethorpe, Ga. She possesses just those qualities that make it possible to have "not fewer than three nor more than nine."

MARY KENNEDY   Vandling, Pa.

Chorus; Y. W. C. A.; Athletic Club.

Mary is always just the same.
Would we had her grace when at a dance!
So artistic, so petite
From her head down to her feet.
For twinkling eyes just take a good glance.

68

MAE LANDON   Canton, Pa.

Y. W. C. A.

Small? Yes, but becomingly so and yet we have
to look up to Mae. Like postum—"there's a reason". Her remarkable dispositon and her singing
voice have good qualities. Ask her "roomie" if
she doesn't strum a wicked uke. Short-stop in baseball must have originated last year when Mae
played. Boy friends? Listen! Mae's folks were on
a party line and the neighbors "kicked" because they
couldn't get any work done.

DANGMAR LARSON   Galeton, Pa.

Y. W. C. A.

Dangmar has proved her right as one of Mansfield's sweetest girls by reason of her sunny disposition and by her winning smiles and ways. Many
persons will find a pleasant recollection in their
Memory Book when they turn back to the page
headed "Your friend Dangmar."

LORETTA LEWIS   Wilkes-Barre, Pa.
                    "RETA"

Athletic Club; Y. W. C. A.; Hiking Club.

Do you know where there is a thrill available?
Tell "Reta", for she's always on the lookout for one.
Every spear of her bobbed hair will curl up with
excitement at the thought of something doing
whether it's a dance, a man, a feed, or a cut.

69

MAE LIGHT   Rush, Pa.
"MAE"
Y. W. C. A.; Hiking Club; Student Council.

We first met Mae on the baseball diamond
pitching a ball. She really is inclined to be an
athlete, at least one would think so when one sees
her shooting baskets from the middle of the gym
floor. Though she sports two deep dimples, we know
she can be serious.

MARY LILLIBRIDGE   Smethport, Pa.
"LIL"
Athletic Club; Y. W. C. A.

Quick, spirited, witty, interesting and interested, this describes "Lil". If you want to get a
fine reward for a little coaxing, just tease Mary to
sing to you. As a student Mansfield admired you,
as a musician she enjoyed you, but as a pal we
treasured you.

FLORENCE LUNDY   Wysox Pa.
"FLOSSIE"
Y. W. C. A.

Curly hair, rosy cheeks and a pleasant smile,
that is Florence. She is a true friend to everybody,
and is always ready to undertake anything that
might come her way. Her first year she was at
Beach Annex.

MARIAN LYON   Elmira, N. Y.

   Art Club (2); *Y. W. C. A.*

   An artist, a student, and a good sport is
Marion, another "Beachnut" worthy of the name.
We are not surprised that the children all love their
teacher. The children are not alone in their adoration. For confidential information send self-
addressed stamped envelope to Williamsport,
Marian's "city of dreams."

SARAH MAC LEAN   Galeton, Pa.
                   "SALLY"

   Orchestra (1) (3); *Glee Club* (1); *Y. W. C. A.*

   If you haven't become acquainted with "Sally",
it's your own ill luck. Her motto is "Do your best
and don't worry." She is always ready for a good
time, but willing to lend a sympathetic hand. May
the best of luck be yours, "Sally", in whatever
you do.

BERTHA MASTERS   Hornell, N. Y.

   This tall girl drops her r's and what a musical
voice she has. We're ready to listen to Bertha any
time. She is also an excellent student and furnishes
many fine "idears" in her classes. By the way, did
you see "The Challenge", a very fine composition
which Bertha wrote?

71

MARY McCONNELL   Mansfield, Pa.

Mary by name and nature. We are safe in
saying that she is always happy, sometimes frivolous
and never anything but entertaining and refreshing.
In looking at Mary you are conscious of a pair of
very dark brown eyes looking straight-forwardly at
you. In all Mary is a type rarely found.

LEAH MERRICK   Mansfield, Pa.

"LEE"

Insatiable is her thirst for knowledge and
boundless the field of her endeavor. All she undertakes is marked by purpose, power and ultimate
perfection. "Lee" is not so inhuman as this description might imply. There are human instincts within
her that have made her the best kind of a pal to
us all.   .

MARY MILOTA   Forest City, Pa.

*Y. W. C. A.; Rurban Club; Emersonian Liter-
ary Society.*

Mary is Mansfield's "Champion Penman". She
has received not less than five diplomas and is still
working for more. Ornamental penmanship is her
chief hobby. We hope that some day she will be a
great penman.

Mary is very studious and so quiet you would
scarcely know she is here.

HELEN MINKLER Little Meadows, Pa.
"MINK"

Athletic Club; Hiking Club; Y. W. C. A.

Creature of impulse—laughing, happy, and gay. "Never serious?" you say. Those who know her best know that under the laughter and fun lies earnestness, generosity, and a sympathetic understanding of human nature.

HILMA MISSIMER Jersey Shore, Pa.

Y. W. C. A.; Hiking Club.

An interesting, lively girl is Hilma. Her eyes sparkling with merry mischief and the smile lurking close to the surface, disclose the fact that fun is hidden around wherever she goes. Yes, Hilma is unique in personality and abilities.

ANN MORAN Genesee, Pa.
"IRISH"

Athletic Club; Y. W. C. A.; Emersonian Literary Society.

Here's a motto just her fit:
"When you think you've trouble hit,
    Laugh a bit.
All the shadows off will flit
If you have the grit and wit
Just to laugh a little bit."

73

ESTHER MORGAN   Old Forge, Pa.

Calm and unruffled, Esther has spent two years
in our midst. When all the rest of us have been
ravaged by the siege of books and teaching, Esther
has appeared cool and collected, without a hair mis-
placed, and with her work all done and O. K. And
yet she has time on the side to do almost anything
that suits her fancy.

MARGUERITE MURPHY   Kingston, Pa.
                "PEGGY"

Marguerite is noted for her reserve; a reserve
that approaches almost to shyness. However, if you
can get beyond this outward personality, it is well
worth the trouble. Quite and sincere, she is a
pleasant contrast to some of the more loquacious,
though well-meaning daughters of '29·

HELEN NIVISON   Cedar Run, Pa.
                ' TINY"

Y. W. C. A.; Hiking Club.

The characterization "short and snappy" fits
Helen. Here we have a brilliant ray of all the sunshine of our class. Her presence in a group always
brings cheerfulness and pleasure and she is warmly
welcomed wherever she appears. Her disposition,
attitude and manners all merge into one word, sincerity.

STELLA NOWAKOWSKI   Blossburg, Pa.

A giggle, a few excited words, and then a silence—we know by her merry eyes that her classes are over and she is ready to catch the bus for "Bloss." Stella is always ready to go home; however, she is anxious to have her work done accurately before she leaves. Anyone as eager as Stella will surely succeed.

DOROTHY O'CALLAHAN   Susquehanna, Pa.
                    "DOT"
Athletic Club.

"Let us care more for serving than winning."

This seems to be "Dot's" creed. Just to meet "Dot" makes you feel good. Her winsome smile and friendly greeting have made her a friend to everyone at M. S. T. C. An attractive girl with such a cheery disposition, with so much pep and enthusiasm is hard to find. Mansfield will miss her. I wonder,— will she make a success? Why mention it? The teaching profession needs many more just like her.

MARGARET R. O'MALIA   Wilkes-Barre, Pa.
                "PEJJIE"
Y. W. C. A.; Athletic Club; Freshman Decoration Committee; Senior Decoration Committee.

One of the hardest tasks in the world is that of paying tribute to a friend. We undertake this task for "Pejjie" with efforts we deem puny, though exceedingly well meant. "Pejjie" is one of those rare characters with the extra something, auburn hair, exquisite, beautiful. lithesome, graceful, keen-witted, dramatic, a diamond of the first water. Though she has been a scintillating enigma for two years we proffer our friendship at her feet.

75

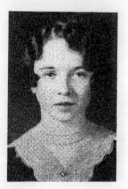

75

JULIA ORR   Sayre, Pa.

Y. W. C. A.

Julia's evident goal is to become a primary
teacher. Toward this goal she has progressed
rapidly which is shown by her success as a "scrub"
in Wellsboro's second grade. Her ability secured
for her a place in the Art Club, and her character,
a place in our memories.

LEON PALMER   *Canton, Pa.*

Quiet and shy, it was some time before Leon
made himself known; and even now he is rather an
enigma to many. He usually can be found at his
desk absorbing knowledge. Many a time he has held
his own when one of his erring classmates have
attempted to disturb him.

MARTHA PERSING   Allenwood, Pa.
                "MARTIE"

Y. W. C. A.

Martha is just a little girl, but we never see her
without a smile. We always wondered why she was
so happy, until one day she gave herself away by
talking about "Bill".
"Man! Thou pendulum betwixt a smile and tear."

ISABEL POKORNY   Wilkes-Barre, Pa.

"IZZY-POKE"

Art Club; Y. W. C. A.

Anyone who knows "Izzy" (and we all do) can say that she is popular with everyone. She is a typical blonde; and we know that , "One blonde hair can draw more than a hundred pair of oxen."

As a teacher we know that she will make good because her student-teaching has been a success, both at Mansfield and at Wellsboro.

BELLE POTTER   Sugar Run, Pa.

Y. W. C. A.

"Nothing is impossible to industry."

Belle is one of those girls who came to college to acquire knowledge and who will be able to do her duty as a teacher. She is liked by all who know her.

GRACE PYNE   Wyoming, Pa.

Vice President of Outdoor Club; Y. W. C. A.; Glee Club.

Gracious ....Yes
Real ....Very
Artistic ....Truly
Carefree ....Slightly
Energetic ....Extremely
Pastime ....Dancing
Young ....Pleasingly
Neat ....Surely
Exceptional ....Very
That's she.

AMY REESE   Blossburg, Pa.

Y. W. C. A.

Amy is a very talented young lady who comes to us every day from Blossburg. With her witty speeches she surely makes the Day Room a lively place. Is there anyone who hasn't heard her play the piano or sing? Well, if there is such a person, he certainly has missed a treat. Although Amy is preparing for the teaching profession, she expects to make her home in Chicago.

WANYTTA REINWALD   Wellsboro, Pa.

Hiking Club; Y. W. C. A.; Tribunal; Athletic Club; Emersonian Literary Society.

Never a slow easy drawl won more friends than hers—and you'd better be careful, or her smile will take you unawares! Then, too, you know she dances well, plays tennis well, skates well—does everything well in fact. And with it all she is a veritable "Spirit of Independence."

SARAH V. RIPLEY   Gaines, Pa.

Y. W. C. A:

Sarah was here in 1926 for one term, but went back to scatter some seeds of knowledge among the youth of Gaines in 1927. This year she is again among us with her quaint happy giggles and her pleasant smile for everyone.

HAROLD ROBINSON   Rummerfield, Pa.

Harold moves in a quiet, peaceful manner; nothing seems to worry him or to hurry him. He is a man of experience. "Experience joined with common sense is a providence to mortals."

RUTH H. ROLAND   Taylor, Pa.
                "SOPHIE"

Y. W. C. A. (1) (2); *Rurban Club* (2); *Athletic Club*.

"Sophie" comes from Taylor and that brands her as a member of the "Fourth Floor Hospital Suite". Her biggest problem since she came to Mansfield has been to decide whether to spend her vacations at Hyde Park or Taylor. She finally arranged to spend Wednesday and Sunday in Taylor. Perhaps "Clarky" figures in this arrangement— but then "Clarky" has a keen liking for poetry and so has Ruth.

FLOSSIE ROSENGRANT   Tunkhannock, Pa.
                "FLO"
Hiking Club.
Those who don't know Flossie think that she is very quiet and reserved, but just ask the girls who knew her when she stayed in the dorm. She is very studious and ambitious and a whiz at basketball.

IOLA ROUPP   Liberty, Pa.

Iola came to us with two years of actual school teaching experience. Her perseverance and conscientious attitude show that college means more than a mere certificate. Sincerity and dependability, make her a friend in the real sense of the word.

ELIZABETH ROWE   Ulster, Pa.

Outdoor Club.

Serious, sensible, solemn, jolly, and reserved— she is a staunch friend, and a good exact workman. Her smile has an irresistible charm which makes her the kind of a girl we like to have around in cloudy weather.

MYRTLE RUMSEY   Gillett, Pa.
                        "TONY"

Hiking Club.

"Tony"? Ah, yes, now we have one that is entirely different. Here is a girl who is quiet and dignified one moment, and laughing and gay the next. "Tony" is fond of dancing and good-looking fellows. Her favorite song is "My Little Indian Man".

Mary Rymkiewicz   Wilkes-Barre, Pa.

'"MOLLY"

*Cecelian Glee Club; Art Club; Y. W. C. A.;
Emersonian Literary Society; Athletic Club.*

"Nothing but death could part me from my
dignity."

Tall and debonair, combined with good looks
and charming ways is our Mary. Mary is always
ready for a good time, and is an all-round good
sport. We are sure she will succeed as a teacher if
she will follow the profession—but we sometimes
wonder.

Winifred Schanbacher   Mansfield, Pa.

"WINNIE"

Beware of her golden hair! This fair lassie is
worth her weight in gold. She is a radiant beam of
sunshine to her hosts of friends. "Winnie" is an
ever-ready and eternal pal. It's the things she has
done, the deeds she has done, and the tasks accomplished that give us the accurate value of her.

Betty Schnell   Plymouth, Pa.

Y. W. C. A.; Athletic Club.

"She's got eyes of blue and that's Bill's weakness now." Betty entered college with the idea that
men were out of her line—but men will break
through lines.

And Bill, like Caesar, "Came, saw"—but we have
our doubts as to whether anyone will ever "conquer."

BETTY SCHULTZ   Kingston, Pa.

*Hiking   Club;   Outdoor   Club;   Emersonian
Society.*

Betty can talk the long night through,
On friends, on books, gowns, and chapeaus, too,
On etiquette so proper,
On teas you can't stop her;
Once Betty's started her words will not be few.

GERTRUDE SCHWASNICK   *Coudersport, Pa.*

Athletic Club (1) (2).

"Gertie" takes her work and her friends seriously. She likes to have her friends with her at all
times and if they don't come to her she hunts them
up.

If you wish to hear an interesting tale ask
'Gertie" to tell you about her visit in New York
last summer.

ELIZABETH B. SEAL   New Milford, Pa.

Y. W. C. A. (1) ; *Y. W. C.* A. *Cabinet* (1) (2);
Art Club (1) (2); *Glee Club* (1); *Outdoor Club*
(1); *Rurban Club* (2);

Betty is one of the famous Seal sisters who
keep things going on "Fourth". Baseball, hiking,
dancing, and eating are a few of Betty's weaknesses;
and that does not include those week-end trips to
J. C.

MILDRED F. SEAL   New Milford, Pa.
"MILLY"

Y. W. C. A. (1); Y. W. C. A. Cabinet (2); Art
Club (1) (2); Glee Club (1); Outdoor Club (1);
Rurban Club (2).

Milly reminds us so much of the old-fashioned
girl that we can readily imagine her sitting in one
of those old-fashioned gardens among the roses. This
casts no reflections on Milly's mirror of life, however. We know that anyone with as sweet and
reserved a manner as "Milly" is bound to be
a success in life.

MATHILDE SEAMAN   Williamsport, Pa.

Dark hair and eyes—and what eyes! An
affinity for dancing, tennis, and what not—a marked
ability to imitate people. By the way, did you ever
hear her talk? If you did, and didn't fall for her
charm, you must have had some kind of a complex.

MARY SECHRIST   Roaring Branch, Pa.

Mary is one of those girls that one can't easily
forget, because of her jolly spirit and willingness to
help others. Mary is very studious and takes her
work seriously. She is a deep thinker and possesses
an analytical mind. Mary has well chosen her profession for she had great success in her two years'
teaching.

83

MARY SHAUT   Canisteo, N. Y.

Nero may have fiddled while Rome burned, but had Mary been the high potentate, a smile would have been in order. Providence knew what was best for us when it sent us Mary, this versatile girl with the winning personality.

JULIA SHEARER   Wyalusing, Pa.

"JUDY ANN"

Y. W. C. A.

"Sweets to the sweet."

No wonder Julia received so much candy, but that necessitated her walking every day to keep slim, and often she "Ransom".

Julia makes few mistakes, but her most glaring one is getting in the wrong room; however, smallest errors are always the best.

MARIAN SHEEN   Elkland, Pa.

Glee Club (1); *Y. W. C. A.* (2).

"She frames her mind to mirth and merriment which bears a thousand charms and lengthens life."

We have seen Marian here many more week-ends this year than last. We are glad that she finds Mansfield more attractive.

PAULINE SIGLER   Wyalusing, Pa.
"PEENIE"
Y. W. C. A.

"She's quiet to those who don't know her well,
But, oh, her friends, what they could tell."

"Peenie" believes the room needs a good cleaning
every two weeks and that it's the room-mate's turn.
"Home, Sweet Home" is one of her mottoes. Hockey,
music, and ??? are her weaknesses. She is a loyal
friend and an all around good sport.

ALBERTA R. SIMRELL   Factoryville, Pa.
"AL"

Y. W. C. A. (1) (2); *Glee Club* (1); *Orchestra*
(1) (2); *Rurban Club* (2).

"Al" is one of those girls whom people do not
forget, whether the sex be male or female. We know
that one who has as charming a personality as "Al"
is capable of other things besides the pleasures and
frivolities of life. We wish you barrels of success,
"Al"!

NELLIE SIZER   Allentown, N. Y.

"Care to our coffin adds a nail, no doubt
And every grin so merry, draws one out."

This is Nellie's motto. Leave it to Nellie to
enjoy herself wherever she is—pretty, peppy,
enthusiastic, with a personality all her own.

85

FLORENCE SLINGERLAND   Troy, Pa.

"That silence is one of the great arts of conversation is allowed by Cicero himself, who says, there is not only an art, but even eloquence in it."

GRACE A. SMITH   Addison, N. Y.

Class Treasurer (1); *Glee Club* (1); *Hockey* (1) (2); *Athletic Club* (1) (2); *Dramatic Club* (2); *Cheer Leader* (2).

If "Scotty" had been a man, she'd have joined the National Guard, but being a girl, she did the next best thing. An' brother! You should hear her give commands.

"G. A. S." spells gas we know, but it means "Grace"—with ability and sincerity—in full measure.

MABEL SMITH   Milan, Pa.
"CAP"

Y. W. C. A. (1); *Athletic* (2); *Hiking Club* (1); *Outdoor Club* (1).

Favorite pastime: "Thinking of Paris."
Favorite Saying: "Dry Humor, I call it."
Favorite Song: "Blue Skies."
"Eat, drink and be merry, for tomorrow you die." "Cap" lives up to this motto by her clever sayings and her keen sense of humor. She is well-known as one of "The Three Musketeers."

86

THYRA SMITH   Wellsboro, Pa.
                "SMITTY"

Athletic Club; Y. W. C. A.

Can she play tennis—and how? "Smitty" on a
tennis court is just one flash of activity, but when
the war is over we see her as just an attractive
blonde with a disarming smile. Perhaps the best
thing we can say of her is that she's a real sport.

HELEN SNYDER   Montrose, Pa.

Hiking Club; Y. W. C. A.; Rurban Club.

"The finest eloquence is that which gets things
done."

If you can catch Helen Snyder without a smile
you are luckier than most of us. As president of
the Summer Council, she proved herself to be most
efficient. Although she has only been here one winter,
we have learned to know and love her.

MAXINE SPRY   Plymouth, Pa.

*Dramatic Club; Athletic Club; Emersonian
Literary Society; Y. W. C. A.*

'Max"—just give us time and we'll tell you
all about her. We can't quite do that but it is our
private opinion that is the original reason why
college men don't always study. A justly famous
"Beachnut", with the ability to accomplish much in
this old world.

87

LULA STEELE   Wellsboro, Pa.
                    "LU"

"Lu" is another of the Wellsboro girls who
grace the dayroom. She is one of the good-natured
variety, always singing and happy. Only the gang
that spends so many happy hours with her can
appreciate her good nature. We surely wish you
much success in teaching "Lu."

EMMA STERLING   Morris Run, Pa.
                    "EM"
Y. W. C. A.

Wouldn't you know that it's Emma Jane who is
at hand at teas and feeds? Wouldn't you know that
it's "Em" with her bright smile and cheery greeting
for all, who can take a joke with such good humor?
Her fondness for children will make her a success
in teaching.

HANA THOMAS   Taylor, Pa.

Rurban Club; Y. W. C. A. (1) (2).

Hana is a rather quiet looking little girl, but, oh
how she can talk! Her cheerful disposition and
amiable personality have won for her many friends
—especially one in Scranton. Maybe, she'll be a
teacher, and then perhaps she won't. She surely has
the ability to capture the A's.

DOROTHY TOMPKINS   Tunkhannock, Pa.

"DOT"

Y. W. C. A.

Everyone knows "Dot", and what is more to the point, everyone likes her. Her unfailing optimism, the light, humorous way in which she takes everything, including life, makes her distinctive and marks her as a gloom-chaser.

MARY THOMPSON   Syracuse, N. Y.

Dramatic Club; Y. W. C. A.; Athletic Club.

"Tommie" came to us this year from Syracuse. Mansfield certainly scored one point on Syracuse that time. She has many talents—dramatic and otherwise. But, so far as we have been able to discover, her ambition is to learn to do the "varsity drag" on a tight rope in her sleep.

EDMUND TUTON   Gillett, Pa.

Rurban Club, President.

The person who said, "Nobody loves a fat man," didn't know "Eddie", we are sure. At least it is of minor importance when we discuss this pleasant individual. He has a way of talking to you so that you think you have known him for years, and after it's over you feel you want to know him all the rest of your years.

JOHN UPDIKE   Gillett, Pa.

Orchestra.

"There is not one virtue so strong as good nature."

Did anyone ever see John "peeved"? We dare say you haven't He has that excellent quality of always being the same to everyone. John has been known to "Chase" to Gillett during the week—wonder why?

SARAH VAN DUSEN   Osceola, Pa.
                    "SALLY"

Y. W. C. A. (2).

"A face with gladness overspread
Soft smiles, by human kindness bred."

We thank Osceola for this contribution to Mansfield State Teachers College. Sally has an exceptionally pleasing personality. Her giggle is one of the outstanding features of the fifth floor "Hospital Gang." All these things have won her many friends.

SARA VAN NESS   Camptown, Pa.
                    "SALLY"

If "Sally" ever once slipped from the straight and narrow path in her two years at Mansfield State, nobody has ever been able to discover it. Who of us, if we did our work as thoroughly and had as obliging a disposition, would not look every day for those little wings which are sure to grow?

GRAYCE VOORHEES Shinglehouse, Pa.

Y. W. C. A.

She's grácious, as the name she holds, implies;
She's friendly as we wish all girls at school would be.
We know she'll do her best in each endeavor,
And prove her worth wherever she may go;
Mansfield State is lucky to have known her
And when she leaves, we all will miss her so.

BLANCHE WALSH Susquehanna, Pa.

"When things go wrong as they sometimes will,
When the road you're treading seems all up hill,
When care is pressing you down a bit,
Rest if you must—but don't you quit."
    This describes Blanche. She loves to teach the
training school children and will surely succeed.

CHRISTINE WALTER Milan, Pa.

"CHRIS"

    A bobbed and bobbing head, snapping brown
eyes, extreme thinness, traveling on high every
minute—that's "Chris". Yet she aspires to dignity,
and no doubt we shall some day hear of "Chris" as
an efficient teacher, for there are vague indications
that she has a serious side.

HELEN WALTERS   Clarks Summit, Pa.
"PAT"

Y. W. C. A.; Outdoor Club.

Helen has individuality. Always ready with an answer—a keen mind is hers. Serious brown eyes, a ready smile, our best wishes, these, too, are hers.

RALPH WARBURTON   Granville Summit, Pa.

Ralph is distinguished by his cheerful personality and keen sense of humor. He is most happy when teasing some of his classmates. When this chap is on the scene you may expect something to be forthcoming. Ralph, always industrious in his efforts, is climbing the ladder to success .

NELLIE MAE WARD   Gillett, Pa.
"NELL"

Y. W. C. A.; Hiking Club; Glee Club.

"A merry heart doeth good like a medicine." Nell's motto. She succeeds well in making the part of the world with which she comes in contact, laugh by her wit and her good humor.

92

SUSAN WHEELER   Olyphant, Pa.

"SUSIE"

Here is Susie, our studious fifth floor representative. She is faithful to her friends and always
willing to help anyone in distress. If you ever feel
hungry, just go to Room 554 and there you will find
an apple. She is a good all around sport.

SYBIL E. WILLIAMS   Plains, Pa.

Glee Club (1); *Y. W. C. A.* (1) (2)! *Hiking
Club* (1) (2).

Sybil, to some people seems to possess a masculine temperament, but deep in her heart she has a
love for femininity.

Her favorite pastime is reading and her main
ambition is to travel. We know she'll be a great
success as a teacher, due to her love of children.

VIOLA WILLIAMS   Ithaca, N. Y.

Y. W. C. A.; Rurban Club.

"Silence is the element in which great things
fashion themselves together; that at length they may
emerge, full-formed and majestic, into the daylight
of life."

A more gracious, kind, courageous and true
friend is not available.

MARIAN WITUCKI   Blossburg, Pa.

One of the Blossburg gang and a great favorite in the Day Room. This is Marian. If you want to know a good sport look her up.

MARGARET WOODWARD   Plains, Pa.
"PEG"

Glee Club (1); *Hiking Club; Athletic Club; Y. W. C. A.*

"Peg" is a member of the well-known "Plains Gang" and Plains has good reason to be proud of such a representative. Quiet, reserved, with the sweetest personality ever, is "Peg". Did you ever hear her sing? Then just visit Room 555 and get the treat of your life.

MARGARET YOUMANS   Mansfield, Pa.

She is "smiling always with a never fading serenity of countenance, and flourishing in an immortal youth." Margaret has a philosophy all her own. It is: "I want to be happy, I have a right to be happy, and it all depends on myself." To such a girl, life surely will be generous.

Juniors

The Junior Class

*E*ARLY IN THE MONTH of September, 1926, there arrived in Mansfield the makings of another period in the history of the State Normal School. The material, that was to furnish an object for the possible penetration of education, passed in state to those eastern hill buildings which were to be their home for some few years. Grim reality here and there had a part in the scene, but "do or die" helped overcome the uncertainty of the new environment and before long life began to regain its natural color. And then came the test of the new-comers, the ordeal that finds the worthy, while those privileged as spectators enjoyed the sport. When thus duly tried and found acceptable, the existence of a Freshman Class in the little world of Mansfield was afforded recognition.

Interest in the novelty of the situation soon subsided and the elements in the process of evolution were allowed freedom of circulation. Little occurred to interrupt the routine of the day until rumors of the possibility of a change of the school's name and status began to spread. Much favorable comment and criticism served to increase interest in that new development, and thus the stage was all set for the ceremonies. By virtue of qualifications recognized by the state, Mansfield was elevated to a position of collegiate standing and accordingly authorized to issue degrees. The right to change the name was withheld, allowing only a suffix if it were desired. With the addition of a new incentive, the Frosh followed through the year, drawing approval to themselves in their one social endeavor of the season, as well as in scholastic ability.

As Sophomores, relative positions changed and the attempt to welcome the Frosh was little short of a grand success. But when too much of self-approval resulted in undesirable estimations, a word to the wise was sufficient. However, after a short delay for re-acclimation, a new stride set in motion the earnest endeavors for improvement. And in the midst of the struggle the school became possessed of a Teachers College title, stock went up several points, but news of the abandoning of Alumni Hall set back the rising hopes. The gymnasium could not hope to accommodate auditorium programs, but visions of a new addition to the campus satisfied any misgivings. While change did its part to improve the value of the school, times rushed along, carrying with it news of the approaching feature. History repeated itself with a will, and records exhibited another start for the promising Sophs.

And now we come to the present Junior Class at Mansfield State, whose growth has followed so closely the development of the school. Many influences have played their part, combined with the survival of the fittest, and the chosen few continue at the task of bravely carrying on the work of a class. Due to a variety of reasons the length of the scroll is less than that of previous years. The powers behind it all has dealt out the hands. To some, it has meant graduating and accepting of wider responsibilities; to others, Dame Fortune has somehow omitted that sideward glance and the head is turned toward some other goal. But those who have been permitted to follow up the fine start still carry on the proud bearing of the class. Quantity and quality are only relative standards, and the task for this class is to balance the scales of achievement by producing a quality measure much superior to that which might support the old saying that "there is strength in numbers."

The completion of this year's program means the passing of the three quarter mark. Whether or not there is to be a realization of those hopes and ambitions of Freshman days is fairly well decided. It is now the time for the uncovering of the sham of youngsters and the shining forth of the real self. Another year will endow these laborers with the privileged rank of Seniors when the lessons of school days meet their capitalization.

JUNIOR CLASS OFFICERS
::

Harry Scholl
President

Dorothy Greene
Secretary

Dr. McNair
Faculty Advisor

Carlton Jackson
Historian

Betty Green
Vice President

Lewis Higley
Treasurer

Junior Class Roll

AVERY, LLOYD D.   "Joe"   WEBSTER, MASS.
"Joe" knows where the good schools are located, for he came all the way from the Plymouth land to attend Mansfield State.

BALCOM, LOIS E.   BINGHAMTON, N. Y.
This golden haired lassie can do anything with a pencil, or a palette and brush. The evidence is shown in the plates of this book.

BARACCO, ORLANDO I.   "Lundy"   ELKLAND, PA.
The Michael Angelo of the Junior Class; otherwise, a likable and learned individual, capable of attaining the height in scholarship and in art.

BEACH, HARRY R.   "Beach"   MANSFIELD, PA.
Never has this notorious collegiate gentleman failed in doing what came his way.

BEACH, HELEN H.   MANSFIELD, PA.
Ready to work, ready to play,
Ready to help you in any way.
Puts this fair damsel on the map

BENSON, DONALD H.   'Don'   MANSFIELD, PA.
Though preparing to assume the teacher's role, Don may become affiliated with chain stores. Envy him, but we must honor his fine abilities.

BIESECKER, ZIDA E.   "Zip"   CLARKS SUMMIT, PA.
"She is gamesome and good, and of likable mood.—
No dreary repeater now and again,
She will be all things to all men."

BOWER, LEIGH H.   NELSON, PA.
A lad of aptitude and profound insight in the fields of science. It is rumored that he is doing extensive research over the week-ends.

BRADSHAW, EDWARD H.   "Ed"   LAWRENCEVILLE, PA.
A quiet man of varied accomplishments—scholastic, dramatic, and executive. Always displaying a smile, his cheerful disposition wins for him many friends.

BRIGGS, CLARENCE F.   MANSFIELD, PA.
At this writing, we salute the only benedict of the Class of '30. He is also noted for his prowess as a wrestler.

BRIHAM. EDWIN D.   "Ed"   TIOGA, PA.
"Ed" may appear quiet and unassuming, but you don't know him, for he is as gay and carefree as the next fellow.

BURROW, DORIS   "Dolly"   VANDLING, PA.
Just another girl from the coal regions,—one look at her hair shows that. Can "Dolly" appreciate a good joke?

CIMBAL, ANTHONY J.   "Tony"   GLEN LYON, PA.
"E Pluribus Unum, sic semper tryannus velocipedus cometatus with a tomatus!" Tony is a classical scholar—he knows his Latin.

CARD, GERTRUDE   "Gert"   ROULETTE, PA.
"Gert" became so fascinated with Mansfield that she decided to remain and climb higher up the tree of knowledge.

COOKE, GRANTLEY J.   "Cookie"   SUSQUEHANNA, PA.
" 'Tis sweet to love, but oh, how bitter
    To love a girl when her clothes don't fit her."

CRAYTON, FLORA   "Flo"   POWELL, PA.
"Flo's" thirst for knowledge remained unquenched at the end of
two years, so she is staying for her degree in the elementary
field.

DOUGHTON, ALLAN I.   "Dot"   MANSFIELD, PA.
Allan's literary talent has won for him the Editorship of the
Flashlight. A probable Editor of the Carontawan next year.

DURDON, HELEN O.   WYOMING, PA.
Though I have labored, these three years, so long,
I still find a place here as one of the throng.

DURANT, DAISY E.   ATHENS, PA.
Daisy's specialty is Fords. And did you say eats?—try 526. She
doesn't have much to say, but she sure knows her "pickles" and
"jam".

DYKINS, FRANCES E.   "Dyke"   MANSFIELD, PA.
"Let me live in a house by the side of the road and be a friend
to man."

FELTS, HELEN   "Feltsie"   CARBONDALE, PA.
An accomplished hostess is Helen and not only this, but she is
very generous.

GILLETTE, ALLEN W.   "Al"   RIDGEWAY, PA.
He went bankrupt in the razor blade industry, scrubbed "deck"
on "Yim City," U. S. N., but is now a matured boy with a sharp
edge.

GRAY, J. GORDON   "Gord"   ARNOT, PA.
Yeah! He goes to school here. Attends classes and all that,
but socially—must be a girl somewhere else.

GREENE. DOROTHY C.   "Dot."   MANSFIELD, PA.
"Don" can tell you all about "Dot"—if he can't, it's his fault.
She sure knows her studies—and how she loves her Latin!

HACKETT, ELMO K.   WELLSBORO, PA.
Elmo is a versatile gent who enjoys a woman's companionship.

HAGER, THEODORE B.   "Ted"   MANSFIELD, PA,
Another chap from Mansfield studying to be a pedagogue, but
there is something else on his mind. Guess it's all O. K. though.

HALSTEAD, KENNETH O.   "Ken"   FACTORYVILLE, PA.
Blustering, storming around,—that's "Ken" when in the inner
confines of South Hall. Underneath this veneer, you will find
him a mighty fine fellow.

HAYNES, NED B.   "Pewee"   CARTIER, CANADA
This Romeo laughs best all the time. Just 220 pounds of harm-
less sweetness. You'd never know he came from the Frigid Zone.

HIBBARD, EDITH   "Hib"   SAYRE, PA.
Edith's motto: "Let us endeavor so to live that when we come
to die, even the undertaker will be sorry."

HIGLEY, LEWIS R.   "Lew"   BRADFORD, PA.
"Lew" is not seen about the campus very much for he is con-
nected with the local hotel. He handles the class treasury with
the skill of Andrew Mellon.

HOLCOMB, J. NEWTON   "Newt"   CANTON, PA.
Unlike an Englishman, "Newt" enjoys a joke, especially concerning his room-mate. Why run when one can walk—that's he.

HOMET, C. EMERSON   WYALUSING, PA.
What are the young men coming to? Emerson also purchases his clothes on the European plan and gives the tailor a promissory note.

HOWARD, FRANCIS W.   HARRISON VALLEY, PA.
A promising young man from the wilds of Potter county. He has performed successfully the task of keeping the Deans well fed.

HOWARD, INEZ M.   "Inex"   HARRISON VALLEY, PA.
Always willing to help others, always kind, always a true friend, that's Inez. Besides this, she is very artistic and original.

HUBBARD, LAWRENCE D.   "Nubbin"   MANSFIELD, PA.
"Nubbin" used to say, "Women never bother me," but now he says, "What's the use of living if you can't have a little fun."

HURLEY, EULALIA I.   CANTON, PA.
Though I'll still be a teacher, 'twill be with a degree.
Thought I'd finished too soon, so I've come back, you see.

JACKSON, CARLTON J.   MANSFIELD, PA.
Affection can withstand severe storms of vigor, but not a long polar frost of indifference. However, Jackson is liked by all the North Hallites.

JUPENLAZ, MATILDA D.   MANSFIELD, PA.
"But he whose inborn worth his acts commend,
Of gentle soul, to human race a friend."

KACHALA, JOSEPH L.   "Joe"   GLEN LYON, PA.
Joe is in every way a good friend and a fine student. His weakness centers in tripping the light fantastic toe at every gym dance.

KAZMARK, HELEN M.   BLOSSBURG, PA.
Helen is always present unless there's a flat tire on the "little green coupe." We fear she has some attraction in "Bloss."

KENDALL, ELWOOD L. "Tubae"   GRANVILLE SUMMIT, PA.
Besides a student, through and through, he is the best tuba player in school. His name is a slogan for good.

KOCHER, JEAN E.   WILLIAMSPORT, PA.
Jean enjoys a good joke and never is found without her smile. Her brown eyes say much for her personality.

KRUTZECK, ALBERT   "Al"   WESTFIELD, PA.
"Al" comes from Conesus College, Buffalo, and stakes a lot on Mansfield. "Law is power," he says, so we include a promising young lawyer.

LENT, LESLIE M.   "P. J."   MANSFIELD, PA.
Perhaps he's not widely known, but he fills his place. Someone wonders what can keep him out late nights—judging by his mid-day naps.

LUTES, MARIEL A.   TUNKHANNOCK, PA.
Mariel is so quiet that it takes a long while to get acquainted with her but when you do, you have gained a friend indeed.

McGUIRE, EDMUND J.   "Mac"   PERRY, N. Y.
Friendly? Cheerful? Well, we should say, and as wise as Old Solomon. He is known around South Hall as the little wizard.

McKINNEY, LOUISE B.   **HALLSTEAD, PA.**
When she is on a rampage, absence of body is better than presence of mind.

MANNINO, LOUISA M.   "Weez"   **LAWRENCEVILLE, PA.**
"Weez" breezed into Mansfield and danced her way into our hearts. Then by good deeds, happy ways and scholastic attainment she retained our friendship.

MANNIX, MARGARET E.   "Peg"   **TOWANDA, PA.**
"Peg" is so busy, she never finds time enough for sleep. Has she ever been to New York? She alone can tell you.

MARBLE, WILHELMINA F.   **WELLSBORO, PA.**
Reserved, quiet and shy, but she has made many friends for herself during her stay with us.

MARKOWICZ, JOHN F.   **WELLSBORO, PA.**
A very serious minded commuter. He knows why he is here.

MICHELSON, E. SYLVIA   **LUZERNE, PA.**
Who is Sylvia? One day a lass came into our midst and by her winsome smiles, dashing ways, initiative and industry, took our school by storm. She is Sylvia.

MORGAN, MARGARET T.   "Peg"   **NEW MILFORD, PA.**
"For, at best, this one short lifetime is a very fleeting playtime; Why, then, waste an hour thereof?"

MORSE, SAM L.   "Sammie"   **TROY, PA.**
This is our fine little tenor who never fails to please. There's not so much to him, but how that much can dance!

MUDGE, EARL, G.   "Fat"   **MANSFIELD, PA.**
You can pick him as the sturdy guard and we'll let his playing speak for his abilities. It's said that he enjoys a little social athletics, too.

OLEARY, JAMES P.   "Jimmie"   **GILLETT, PA.**
He sure makes a racket with his trumpet, but he lives downtown, so we should worry.

OWEN, PHYLLIS C.   "Phil"   **MANSFIELD, PA.**
"Phil" is full of pep and fun. Dancing, tennis and basketball occupy much of her time, but study is a necessary evil.

PAYNE, ELIZABETH   "Betty"   **WILKESBARRE, PA.**
Who's making all the noise? Oh, yes, it's Betty, of course, trying to beat three others talking. But we would miss her.

PEARSON, MARION E.   **BLOSSBURG, PA.**
Looking for Marion? She's studying. However, she doesn't air her knowledge like some of us who study once in a while or not at all.

POLLOCK, FRANCES J.   **ULSTER, PA.**
We haven't yet found out if she has the temper that goes with red hair—or isn't it red? Here's hoping we don't.

POWERS, M. ELOISE   **MANSFIELD, PA.**
A flower of Mansfield, fragile and fragrant, whose sweetness gladdens and refreshes all who know her.

REYNOLDS, RUTH E.   **TUNKHANNOCK, PA.**
How do some people find time to get their lessons so well and be such good musicians? Ask Ruth and find out.

ROSE, DENZEL S.   "Happy"   MANSFIELD, PA.
Happy by name and happy by nature. He is the guy that makes all the wise cracks.

SCHOLL, HARRY J.   GALETON, PA.
This popular youth comes from Galeton, but due to his great success in football, we will forgive him that.

SQUIER, LESTER B.   "Les"   NICHOLSON, PA.
Physical fitness, fine athletic ability—"Les" fills his big place with a will.

STONIER, RALPH W.   "Stony"   NEW MILFORD, PA.
Study and quotations from Ridpath—that's "Stony". Though coming from Dickinson College, he is loud in his praise of Mansfield State.

STOWE, PHILIPPA F.   TIOGA, PA.
"Gentle of speech, beneficient of mind."

SUTTON, JOHN F.   "Sutt"   BLOSSBURG, PA.
Here is one of our jovial commuters that's well liked by all, but better liked by some than others.

THOMAS, J. EVALYN   "Evie"   CANTON, PA.
"Evie" is never "down in the dumps," which is a decided distinction around North Hall.

THOMAS, MARGARET A.   "Peg"   WARRIOR RUN, PA.
"Peg" has made a name for herself in teaching French. We hope she keeps up the good work.

THOMAS, MARY N.   "Mamie"   ASHLEY, PA.
"Mamie" has been with us three years and has made a host of friends. As President of the Hiking Club, she has shown her efficiency in handling affairs.

TROWBRIDGE, JOHN E.   "Jack"   WESTFIELD, PA.
An embryonic prodigy in many lines; science, athletics, society. The official milk-tester of the institution. A variety of interests prevent his becoming narrow-minded.

VAN DUSEN, DOROTHY   "Dot"   MANSFIELD, PA.
"Dot" is quiet in public, but we wonder what she hides behind that quietness. She always has her work done and plenty of time for recreation.

WEBSTER. BERNICE L.   MANSFIELD, PA.
"So on bravely through rain or shine,
Time has his work and I have mine."

WEDGE, JULIA A.   MIDDLEBURY CENTER, PA.
Can it be that Julia liked us so well that she came back? She is so busy that not many get acquainted with her.

WEEKS, W. BENN   "Bennie"   WESTFIELD, PA.
He's good at tennis, better at basketball, and just about the best about the town at dancing.

WHITE, MARK R.   "Whitey"   GALETON, PA.
Whitey came to Mansfield with the reputation of a big brother to live up to. And we're here to state that he has succeeded.

WHITMER, J. FRANKLIN   "Lefty"   POWELL, PA.
Back with us again after an absence of a year due to a football injury. "Lefty" did his duty this year as assistant coach of football.

WILLIAMS, MILDRED C.   "Milly"   HOP BOTTOM, PA.
If you don't know "Milly," you have missed one of the essentials of Mansfield. Nuff sed!

Home Economics

BLOOMSTER, ROSANNA T.   "Nan"   SMETHPORT, PA.
"One friend of tried value is better than many of no account."
She is a friend worth having and we all know it.

BRACE, LELIA M.   "Brace"   MANSFIELD, PA.
Another one of our conscientious "College Town" students.
Brace devotes a good share of her time to studying—that course
in Sieveology.

BUCK, MARGARET E.   "Marg"   STARRUCCA, PA.
"True friends, like diamonds, are rich and rare." This typifies
"Marg," who brightens many a scene with her extraordinary
supply of wit—not omitting her auburn hair.

BURT, AGNES E.   "Ag"   COUDERSPORT, PA.
"God will not love thee less
Because men love thee more."

BYLER, SARAH E.   MORGANTOWN, PA.
"Perfection consists, not in doing extraordinary things, but in
doing things extraordinarily well."

CARLSON, NELLIE V.   "Vi"   SMETHPORT, PA
Her motto: "What do we live for if not to make the world less
difficult for each other?"

ELLSWORTH, J. LINALYS   "Lin"   SPRINGBORO, PA.
One of our active Junior "Home Ecs" in more ways than one.
We think M. S. T. C. has more than one attraction for Lin.

FOX, LENA S.   HALIFAX, PA.
Once I loved deeply; now I love with a laugh.
The thrill's quite as pleasing, the trouble one half.

GEER, HESTER   "Hes"   COUDERSPORT, PA.
A regular plodder, a conscientious student and worker. She's
always willing to assist others with their difficult tasks in life.

GIALDINI, MARJORIE M.   "Marj."   ATHENS, PA.
"A friend is the first person who comes in after the whole world
has gone out"—that's why "Marj" is always first.

GREEN, ELIZABETH G.   "Betty"   HARRISBURG, PA.
"To many a downhearted fellow, your smile will give a sense
of company."

HINMAN, MARY S.   CLEVELAND, OHIO
Our hundred per cent All-American girl—fifty per cent of snap
and pep for our modern days and fifty per cent of poise, quietness and culture of olden days.

HULSLANDER, EVA J.   "Eve"   TROY, PA.
If you want to personify the word "cute," take our little Eva.
Although she doesn't possess the golden curls, she has a golden
disposition.

LEWIS, GERALDINE M.   "Jerry"   LEROY, PA.
"Jerry" seems to be another of our quiet students, but oh, my
when you get to know her! We hear she is strong for Temple.

LICK, GERTRUDE   "Gert"   EDINBORO, PA.
Here's to "Gert," one of our most studious and conscientious
students. No matter what it is to be done, "Gert" is always
willing to help and do her bit.

LLOYD, KATHERINE E.   "Babe"   WILLIAMSPORT, PA.
Happiness is the only good. "The place to be happy is here. The
time to be happy is now. The way to be happy is to help make
others so."

McGROARTY, AGNES M.   "Ag"   WILKES-BARRE, PA.
"Laugh and the world laughs with you, weep and you weep alone,
For a cheerful grin will let you in where the knocker is never
known."

MEYER, MABLE A.   WILLIAMSPORT, PA.
Here's one who prefers down town to college life. Whenever
artistic talent is demanded, particularly poster making, Mable
is called upon for aid.

ROGERS, LYDIA E.   "Lyd"   EMPORIUM, PA.
"There is danger in too many acquaintances, but he who has a
true friend possesses a treasure more precious than the closest
natural tie."

SCHMID, RUTH E.   "Rufus"   ALLENTOWN, PA.
"May good humor preside when good fellows meet." Humor
always presides when we meet "Rufus."

Music Supervisors

BARTLE, MANDERVILLE   "Mandy"   MANSFIELD, PA.
It seems he likes to graduate from our estimable institution.
What would the orchestra do without him? Everyone likes
"Mandy," especially since he bought his new Ford.

BIDDLE, KATHRYN D.   "Kitty"   DUSHORE, PA.
We all know "Kitty" as the girl who "Bobs" around with a
smiling face when she receives a letter with an "S. C." postmark.

CARPENTER, VIOLA M.   "Carp"   ATHENS, PA.
We wonder why we never see "Carp's" smiling face at week-
ends. There must be some other attraction elsewhere. Who knows?

CHAPMAN, LOIS C.   GENESEE, PA.
A great patroness of the arts—music and printing. Lois is
bright, she knows two meanings for the word "devil" (printer's).

FRENCH, MARY S.   MANSFIELD, PA.
Plenty of pep! Plenty of dance!
Plenty of song! Plenty of prance!—that's Mary.

FURMAN. WINIFRED K.   "Freddie" .   WELLSBORO, PA.
We all know she knows her stuff when it comes to lessons, but
—what about driving? Now, "Freddie," be "frank" and 'fess up!

HAMBLIN, RUTH A.   "Hammie"   TUNKHANNOCK, PA.
The smallest but not the least of the "Three H's." We've heard
"Hammie" likes basket picnics on the campus.

HOLCOMB, FLORENCE A.   "Hokie"   COUDERSPORT, PA.
Having had so much practice at Covington "Hokie" is sure to
make a fine violin teacher (unless she decides to teach trumpet).

HORTON, ALTA H.   "Al"   TOWANDA, PA.
"Laugh, clown, laugh!" "Al" supplies the third year "sups"
with unconcealed mirth. She is going to take up concert work
on the harmonica.

HUSTON, MARION E.   WAVERLY, PA.
Rachmaninoff in person! Also Paul Whiteman! What won-
drous stories a piano can tell when played by Marion.

KOEHLER, ELIZABETH C. "Betty"   NEW FLORENCE, PA.
We thought Sodus Point was a summer resort, but it seems to
be attractive to certain people all seasons of the year. Hurrah
for the "Army!"

KOFOED, WINIFRED M.   "Winnie"   SILVER CREEK, N. Y.
"On with the dance! Let joy be unconfined!' ' An otherwise
hard working "Sup" who gets a lot of fun out of dancing.

LESLIE, NORMA J.   WELLSBORO, PA.
Don't mind Norma, she can't help knowing so much about Harmony. Just watch the "Who's Who" for her in later years.

MOON, GRACE E.   KNOXVILLE, PA.
Moon-guided dreams, "If Mansfield were only large enough to
support an opera company!" Grace could be a prima donna with
her wonderful soprano voice.

OHLMAN, LOUISE   SHAVERTOWN, PA.
Though she lives on fourth, she has to stay on fifth most of the
time to keep the gang straight.

PALMER, H. LOUISE   MANSFIELD, PA.
Music is supposed to be her attraction, but she has much interest
in her car and the postman.

PANTALL, LOIS E.   PUNXSUTAWNEY, PA.
"The mystic beauty of an Arabian night;
The exotic fragrance of a Persian garden;
The subtle charm of the Orient, and
Music like a curve of gold."

PARSON, LUCILLE   WILLIAMSPORT, PA.
"I live for those who love me, for those who know me true,
For the heavens that bend above me, and the good that I can do."

PRUGH, LOUISE   TIOGA, PA.
Here's the girl from Tioga. It must take some initiative to
commute so far every day. Anyway, she is one of the faithful.

ROGERS, DOROTHY E.   "Dot"   ATHENS, PA.
"Dot" promises to be another Paderewski, but State College
may interfere.

SPERRY, CLARE E.   ATHENS, PA.
One of the Music Supervisors who did duty on the Council. A
friend to all.

SUMMERS, HARRY A.   "Sarry"   ROULETTE, PA.
Though the only male survivor of the class, he makes up for
those missing. His limber fingers play a big part in the jazz,
so necessary to him.

WASHBURN, MADELINE L.   EDINBORO, PA.
"With head held high, erect in walk,
With mind alert, direct in talk,
She meets success on every side.
She stands up straight, she's straight inside."

SOPHS

The Sophomore Class

HE CLASS of '31 entered into school life for the year of 1928-29 with all the pep possible to a Sophomore Class which feels the necessity of introducing the membership of an incoming class to their Alma Mater. The members of the Tribunal took charge and the glorious initiation of the class of '32 to Mansfield began nearly as soon as the first prospects arrived. And until the Frosh were really on speaking terms with everyone there was no let-up. Seen from this angle the Frosh must agree that a vote of thanks is due us for being considerate enough of them to give them such a fine introduction to the intricacies of life at M. S. T. C. And then, adding insult to injury, Gilvary's Sophomore squad so badly beat the Frosh cohorts in the annual tilt on the gridiron that every Freshman wore a look on his face for months that would have soured the sweetest of honey.

After being in the center of things so long and also doing a good job in occupying this central position, the Sophomores lived up to their reputation by presenting four sturdy men to Old Mansfield to give her fame on the gridiron. Gilvary, Hartman, Hrycenko and Baker upheld Sophomore honors during the football season and, always true to the colors, they "done things up brown."

The flame of glory, so strong during the football season, faded with us slightly during the winter when cage and court were prominent. The only claim we lay to the honors won by the undefeated team of '28-'29 is the contribution to it from our ranks of Manager Frear and Augustine, who was with us as a Freshman. However, we had our full share of debating honors with Davis, Singer and Bartoo representing us on the debating team.

And next in order comes baseball and more opportunity for the class of '31 to show its metal. In this classy field of athletics Scarcello, Gilvary, Wilkinson, Carpenter and Hrycenko blossomed forth and again we had no cause for shame because of the behavior of our classmates.

As was fitting to a class that began to show its superiority even at the early age of a few weeks when we were Freshmen, we continued to hit the books hard and the instructors—against their wishes—were forced to concede that we weren't so dumb after all. But, of course, we couldn't waste too much time with studies—there was our education to consider. For this reason the officers decided to make the Soph Hop one of the greatest events in the history of social affairs at Mansfield. Consequently on the night of the Hop the Red and Blacks presided on the musical end of the program and from that alone one can see the type of entertainment handed out. This fact, coupled with a few original ideas in the line of decoration and refreshments, and the fact that affairs sponsored by the class of '31 are always successful, fulfilled the wildest dream of the ones who laid out the plans for the Hop.

And now that it is all over we look backward to the time we were Sophomores in M. S. T. C. We look ahead to future years of study and work in Mansfield. And last we wish the graduating class the best success and assure them that the years spent in school with them will always be uppermost in our minds.

111

SOPHOMORE CLASS OFFICERS

::

Gaylord Spencer
President

Irving T. Chatterton
Faculty Advisor

Edgar Frear
Vice President

Elizabeth Jarvis
Secretary

Kenneth Dayton
Historian

Glenn Hammer
Treasurer

Sophomore Class Roll

Baxter, Almon   "Bobo"   Granville Summit, Pa.
"Bobo" says he's from Missouri, via Normal Avenue.

Bailey, Harry   "Hank"   Canton, Pa.
A quiet, studious, well-liked fellow.

Baker, Howard   "Bake"   Port Allegany Pa.
"Bake" has three weaknesses and "women" are all of them.

Bartoo, Leonard   "Len"   Charleston, Pa.
"Len" is an outstanding member of any class-room.

Bennett, Fred   "Freddie"   Mansfield, Pa.
"Freddie" captained our victorious class bone-crushers.

Blanchard, William   "Bill"   Covington, Pa.
A cheer leader from the "Frat" house.

Brace, Kenneth   "Cummins"   Mansfield, Pa.
Another local boy visiting school.

Bradshaw, Charles   "Charlie"   Tioga, Pa.
Much might be said on both sides.

Brennan, Alice   "Shorty"   Elkland, Pa.
A good girl who likes to work.

Broderick, Merrill   "Brod"   Mansfield, Pa.
"Brod" drives his car to the "smithy"—and why?

Campbell, Joseph   "Joe"   Ulster, Pa.
A staunch National Guardsman.

Carpenter, Lowell   "Carp"   Ullysses, Pa.
Once he said he had never been "grassed."

Chamberlain, Lucille   "Cil"   Wyalusing, Pa.
Chamberlain—the incomparable.

Curtis, Helen   "Curtis"   Carbondale, Pa.
"A merry heart doeth good like a medicine."

Davis, Wendell   "Dave"   Taylor, Pa.
Everyone's friend.

Dayton, Kenneth   "Date"   Montrose, Pa.
"Who cares for women?"

Dingler, Leona Jane   "Ding"   Jersey Shore, Pa.
Our idea of a good sport.

Doughton, Margaret   "Peg"   Mansfield, Pa.
A nature perfectly balanced; a beauty of heart untold.

Dunbar, Alonzo   "Al" Columbia Cross Roads, Pa.
"And hereby hangs a tale."

Eighmey, Carol   "Kay"   Mansfield, Pa.
A bushel of fun.

Fisk, Cortez   "Cort"   Wyalusing, Pa.
A hunter brave and bold.

Flaherty, Anne   "Anne"   Pittston, Pa.
Work's good for a person.

Franklin, Albion   "Albumen"   Towanda, Pa.
He's in line for class honors.

Frear, Edgar   "Edjer"   Montrose, Pa.
Our best campus guard.

French, Amy   "Frenchie"   Mansfield, Pa.
A good mixture of attentiveness, pep, and giggles.

Gilchrist, Margaret   "Peg"   Lake Como, Pa.
"A happy smile, a merry word," characterizes "Peg."

Gilvary, William   "Bill"   Jessup, Pa.
Speaking of stars—"Bill" is a planet.

Hartman, Charles   "Mickey"   Susquehanna, Pa.
Another Sophomore playing a stellar role.

Hertz, John   Hertz   Elkland, Pa.
A mighty dependable fellow.

Holly, Hugh   "Holly"   Lawrenceville, Pa.
From Lawrenceville, but all right just the same.

James, Ruth   "Ruthie"   Plains, Pa.
Patience, perseverance, and pep make up Ruth.

Jarvis, Elizabeth   "Liz"   Sayre, Pa.
Carefree, a delicate air, willing to help most anywhere.

Jenkins, Clifford   "Jenks"   Covington, Pa.
The class' best orator.

Jupenlaz, Fred   "Freddie"   Mansfield, Pa.
A mighty fine fellow—always ready to help.

Justin, Raymond   "Justin"   Mansfield, Pa.
Can he sing? And how!

Kelley, Erma   "Kell"   Covington, Pa.
Quiet and resourceful—that's Erma.

Knapp, Eloise   "Snap"   Wolfe Hollow, Pa.
Contrary to the red hair rule—Eloise is easy-going.

Knowlton, Doris   Syracuse, N. Y.
Doris came to us from Syracuse and likes to return home frequently. I wonder.

Lefler, Bernita   "Nita"   Westport, Conn.
Blue eyes, wavy hair, sunny smile, never a care.

Miller, Michael   "Mike"   Duryea, Pa.
Mike runs Frear a close second.

Neefe, Gertrude   "Gert"   Coudersport, Pa.
Just a mighty nice girl.

Novak, Leah   Elkland, Pa.
They're always together. Who? The Elkland gang.

Popadick, Michael   "Mike"   Costello, Pa.
Studious? Perhaps not, but "What does it matter?"

Powers, Gordon   "Gord"   Mansfield, Pa.
"Gord" certainly is studious.

Prugh, Frank   "Pru   Tioga, Pa.
Tioga lost when it sent Frank to us.

Ransom, Vivian   New Milford, Pa.
She lives in a house by the side of the road.

Reinwald, LaVerne   "Reinie"   Wellsboro, Pa.
"The talent of success is nothing more than doing well whatever you do."

Rieppel, Ann   Cowanesque, Pa.
  You should see her play hockey.

Rivenburg, Russell   "Russ"   Clifford, Pa.
  Somehow Russ finds staying down-town very interesting.

Saunders, Ella   Avoca, Pa.
  She likes to study U. S. Government. "Now you tell one."

Scarcello, Angello   "Ange"   Elkland, Pa.
  Elkland surely sent us a fine baseball man.

Schultz, Vernon   "Schultzy" Williamsport, Pa.
  Talented, versatile, amiable.

Seagers, Genevieve   "Gen" Harrison Valley, Pa.
  Nothing's dead when Gen's around to stir it up.

Seeley, Margaret   Emporium, Pa.
  Men may come, men may go, but I go on forever.

Sharpe, Helen   Mehoopany, Pa.
  Here's an example of a nice quiet girl.

Shaw, Daryl   Mansfield, Pa.
  A resolute spirit is the stoutest ally.

Sherman, Harland   "Shermie" Mansfield, Pa.
  "To-day is our own; a fig for to-morrow."

Smith, Renabel   "Rena"   Mansfield, Pa.
  The self starter for the day room gang.

Spencer, Gaylord   "Doc"   Ulysses, Pa.
  Our class president.

Stabler, Eleanor   "Nell" Williamsport, Pa.
  The girl with the never ending line.

Stevens, Arthur   "Art"   Tioga, Pa.
  He is a chemist.

Suhocke, Anthony   "Su"   Kingston, Pa.
  Al Smith's dynamic campaign manager at M. S. T. C.

Sullivan, Alecia   "Lecia" Waverly, N. Y.
  "She has the genius to be loved."

Thomas, Anthony   "Tony"   Wannamie, Pa.
"Tony" Thomas, star tackle of the Sophomores.

Tozer, Ruth   Sayre, Pa.
"Sober, steadfast and demure."

Van Dusen, Hugh   "Van"   Elkland, Pa.
A future Ralph Greenleaf.

Walton, Florence   Montrose, Pa.
Pretty and witty. Who can deny it?

Wilcox, Nelson   "Wilkie"   Muncy, Pa.
A student and a friend. What more could one want?

Wilkinson, Ralph   "Duff"   Wellsboro, Pa.
He can surely trip the light fantastic.

Wingate, Gladys   "Polly"   Wellsboro, Pa.
She's little, but she swings a mean hockey stick.

Winner, Edith   "Weinner"   Colvert, Pa.
She's all her name implies.

Young, Basil   "Basil"   Mansfield, Pa.
Quiet and reserved—that's Basil.

Yurkewitch, Irene   Elkland, Pa.
She keeps the "Shining Lights" stepping.

Music Supervisors

Capwell, Elwood   "Cappy"   Wyalusing, Pa.
Our future trombone virtuoso.

Dibble, Merla   "Dib"   Meshoppen, Pa.
Gentle, timid, sweet, and kind are her attributes defined.

Gilbert, Mary Louise   "Chic"   Millersburg, Pa.
She is what her name implies.

Girton, Martha   "Nan"   Berwick, Pa.
The Jennie Lind of our class.

Gleokler, Dolly   "Dolly" ·   Canton, Pa.
The lass with the delicate air.

Grant, Robert   "Bob"   Mansfield, Pa.
Red head and Scotch and not ashamed of it.

Horne, Pauline   "Hornie"   Johnstown, Pa.
Late, but here forever.

Krivsky, Frank   "Frankie"   Mansfield, Pa.
Frank has been showing us what a violinist really is.

Kiethline, Mildred   "Midge"   Shickshinny, Pa.
Shickshinny's loss is our gain.

Kunkle, Helen   "Kinkle"   Williamsport, Pa.
A quiet room: Slam! Bang! And a giggle! Helen entered.

Hetrick, Louise   "Lou"   Altoona, Pa.
Her friendship is cherished by those who know her best.

Lenkler, Lucille   "Priscilla   Millersburg, Pa.
Meant for opera.

Long, Raymond   "Jack"   Mansfield, Pa.
Valentino—watch your step.

Miller, Frank   "Duke"   Monroeton, Pa.
Duke's delight is waking the boys with his trumpet.

Morandi, Marguerite "Marg"   Tioga, Pa.
She is kind, friendly and unrestrained.

Palmer, Ruth   Trucksville, Pa.
Like a goddess fair and most divinely tall.

Parke, Gilbert   "Parkey"   Waynesburg, Pa.
One of the mainstays of the smokers' quartet.

Parry, Cora   "Pat"   Forest City, Pa.
Like a gleam of sunshine on a cloudy day.

Roderick, Donald   "Don"   Dimock, Pa.
Don is a real leader—even in his quartet work.

Seamans, Waldo   "Seam"   Lawrenceville, Pa.
Our skylark. Sing us "Sonny Boy," "Seam," we like it.

Singer, Letha   "Singer"   Williamsport, Pa.
Laugh and the world laughs with you."

Swatsworth, Ellen   "Swat"   Johnstown, Pa.
Fritz has nothing on her.

Watson, Frederick   "Freddie"   Athens, Pa.
A piano and vocal artist.

Welliver, Carolyn   "Lynn"   Muncy, Pa.
Can she dance? Hey! Hey!

Wendle, Mary   "Becky"   Williamsport, Pa.
Miss Williamsport. Irish? Well, partly, at least.

Wheeler, Gladys   "Gladie"   Clark's Summit, Pa.
Let's be silent, for silence is the speech of love.

Home Economics

Barry, Margaret   "Peg"   White Haven, Pa.
There's a bird on the dollar.

Baumink, Roberta   "Bobs"   Fredonia, N. Y.
But that's no reason why you should let it fly.

Beaver, Julia   "Judie"   Waynesboro, Pa.
Charm strikes the sight, but merit wins the soul.

Brace, Marian   Wyoming, Pa.
A foundation of good cookery is accuracy.

Carey, Bethia   "Beth"   Millville, Pa.
We do not worry about the future of this conscientious lass.

Caswell, Mary   "Mary"   Taylor, Pa.
Smiles and good cooking go together. Ask Mary.

Deatrick, Alice   Scranton, Pa.
The leaders of to-morrow will have to be likable.

Driscoll, Helen   Plymouth, Pa.
Always willing to give time to her friends.

Edgecomb, Ester   "Essie"   Knoxville, Pa.
Melancholy, I's no use for you, by golly.

Gardner, Alice   "Al"   Meshoppen, Pa.
She season's cooking with brains.

Gehron, Florence   "Flossie"   Williamsport, Pa.
The secret of success is concentraton.

Hager, Genevieve   "Gen"   Mansfield, Pa.
Her friendly spirit means much to those who know her.

Hoover, Frances   "Sal"   Williamsport, Pa.
Any time is a good time to start.

Jones, Helen   "Shorty"   Mansfield, Pa.
Ah, but a man's reach should exceed his grasp.

Kickline, Ruth   "Kick"   White Haven, Pa.
Prosperity makes friends, adversity tries them.

Ormsby, Clara   "Caddie"   Bradford, Pa.
I'm inclined to be left handed.

Rice, Catherine   "Kay"   Trucksville, Pa.
Rice is great for weddings.

Rose, Dorothea   "Dot"   Mansfield, Pa.
Don't mind the thorns, rather give thanks for the roses.

Shollenberger, Martha   "Mart"   Williamsport, Pa.
The Home Ecs grow better every day.

Swartz, Helen   "Swartzie"   Waynesboro, Pa.
Regardless of what the self-styled student critics say.

Wood, Myritilla   "Tilly"   Knoxville, Pa.
Did you hear this one? Ask "Tilly" about it.

FROSH

The Freshman Class

STOP! LOOK! LISTEN! Here comes the class of '32. Some classes stand out because of quantity; others, by virtue of quality. A strange body of Freshmen, we, the most humble species of college life, under the weight of heavy baggage, poured sorrowfully into the Halls of Fame that memorable day of 1928 to receive our initiation into the great M. S. T. C. Some of us marched as though we were going to battle, others more brave came in boldly, holding high our heads, but most of us advertised the fifty-seven varieties; very green, awkward and funny. The halls were literally crowded with gauking, gaping "Frosh." We were the object of the seniors raillery— we were the mirth of the Juniors—and the laugh of the sophomores. Everybody acknowledged immediately that the class of '32, approximately three hundred and five in number, distinguished themselves in quantity at least. Ever since we have been proving that we have the quality, too.

The whole college welcomed us with "slams" delivered in that biting tone peculiar to upper classmen when addressing little Freshmen. Some of us witty ones soon learned that it was not etiquette to ridicule that "Stupid Tribunal," as we named it. Under the leadership of four instructors we have taken an active part in our college activities and have now become acclimated.

Our class took its first plunge into society life by inviting the upperclassmen to our "matinee" or dance. In the latter part of the year, the Freshmen girls showed their appreciation to their "Big Sister" by inviting them to their tea. Much originalty and talent were displayed in making the "Freshmen Frolic" and tea unrivalled successes. During the course of our journey we as a class have become distinctive and distinguished not only in an unbeatable reputation in athletics, but in music and scholastics as well. For those musically inclined membership for Freshmen was granted in both the band and orchestra in which some very excellent talent has developed. Almost every activity was opened to us: for the book-worm there has been our library with fiction, history, science; something for each one; for those of us who like sport, behold our football, our basketball, our baseball and our tennis teams; those of us who yearned for the glare of the footlights or desire to follow in the footsteps of Daniel Webster are now members of the Emersonian Society, Rurban Club and Debating Club. Now, our organizations are besprinkled with Freshmen of every description. But, of course, the upperclassmen were not quite ready to receive the adolescents into their confidence and for a short time clouds of disappointment engulfed them. Soon, however, the upper classmen were satisfied that the class was capable of bearing the weight of responsibility which comes with participation in activities and their high hat was stored away. The end of the 1928-'29 road is here. The class steadily forges ahead, and if it continues to do so in the same spirit, we will be by far the most successful class ever graduated at Mansfield State Teachers College.

FRESHMEN CLASS OFFICERS

Ellsworth Allis
President

Marian Marrow
Treasurer

Clifford Balch
Faculty Advisor

Ruth Hoffman
Historian

Errold Wydman
Vice President

Arline Davis
Secretary

Freshman Class Roll

Group Four

allis, ellsworth d. ....snake .... mansfield, pa.

applegate, erva r. ....goldie ....mansfield, pa.

ayres, eugene ....jene ....mansfield, pa.

barner, elizabeth j. ....betty ....towanda, pa.

baynes, harold e. ....baynesie ....mansfield, pa.

biancho, alda l. ....al ....elkland, pa.

billings, guy ....bill ....springville, pa.

blanchard, leo c. ....blanc ....nelson, pa.

brown, theresa a. ....tab ....binghamton, n. y.

bullock, ellen m. ....len .... tunkhannock, pa.

cleveland, nelson g. ....nelt ....mansfield, pa.

corbin, barnett ....corbin ....montour falls, n. y.

curtiss, mary b. ....gillie ....middletown, n. y.

davenport, hilda ....curly ....towanda, pa.

devine, william c. ....bill ....lawton, pa.

doll, elwood l. ....ell ....tunkhannock, pa.

doud, howard r. ....doud ....mansfield, pa.

doughton, anna e. ....ann ....mansfield, pa.

egelston, dorothy m. ....dot ....elkland, pa.

farr, marie e. ....ghinger ....tunkhannock, pa.

french, harriett v. ....kate ....mansfield, pa.

gamble, sara r. ....sally .... williamsport, pa.

gould, alfred ....al ....mansfield, pa.

guiles, mary f. ....gil ....lawrenceville, pa.

hachita, katsutaro m. ....katz ....wilkes-barre, pa.

hardie, alexander m. ....al ....ridgefield park, n. j.

hewitt, catherine j. ....katinka ....blossburg, pa.

hewitt, catherine r. ....kay ....sayre, pa.

hotalen, william d. ....wilt ....mansfield, pa.

hutcheson, richard r. ....dick ....blossburg, pa.

johnson, howard l. ....john ....factoryville, pa.

kusheba, stasia d. ....kush ....glen lyon, pa.

lathrop, bunnell ....bunnie ....springville, pa.

lent, frances a. ....fran ....mansfield, pa.

lewis, gomer ....joe .... jermyn, pa.

lutes, ferris f. ....awk ....mansfield, pa.

mallalieu, eleanor l. ....nara ....williamsport, pa.

marvin, tena a. ....tene ....covington, pa.

moore, floyd m. ....duke ....mansfield, pa.

moyer, wilton j ....will ....galeton, pa.

norbert, alexander a. ....al ....kingston, pa.

obourn, herman h. ....pat ....mansfield, pa.

painter, louise j. ....tinker ....corning, n. y.

pelegrino, pete m. ....pellie ....galeton, pa.

pish, martin e. ....midget ....olyphant, pa.

pogar, elmore e. ....pogar ....noxen, pa.

raker, miles f. ....raker ....liberty, pa.

reinwald, mary ....reiny ....wellsboro, pa.

schroeder, margaret h. ....peggie ....wilkes-barre, pa.

scudder, louise j. .... lou ....cooper's plains, n. y.

sheeby, mary a. ....schinny ....binghamton, n. y.

shoemaker, pauline m. ....polly ....canton, pa.

simms, frank ....ricky ....scranton, pa.

smith, r. gould ....smitty ....halstead, pa.

smith, leonard a. ....smith-brat ....montrose, pa.

snyder, h. austin ....snyder ....waymart, pa.

spencer, raymond m ....ray ....lambs creek, pa.

stevens, m. elizabeth ....beth ....wellsboro, pa.

terry, george h. ....red ....new albany, pa.

titus, pauline m. ....polly ....tunkhannock, pa.

trevitt, william a. ....willow ....jermyn, pa.

van dusen, regina ....van ....mansfield, pa.

verbeck, gladys m. ....glad ....troy, pa.

vosburg, ernest k. ....erny ....mansfield, pa.

webster, dorothy ....dot ....mansfield, pa.

webster, walter s. ....walt ....wellsboro, pa.

wheeler, j. ward ....mose ....mansfield, pa.

whittaker, glen h. ....whitty ....mansfield, pa.

wolfe, edna l. ....eddie ....snedekerville, pa.

wydman, frank e. ....wydie ....corning, n. y.

Groups One and Two

ameigh, mary e. ....betty ....gillett, pa.

antes, evelyn m. ....kicker ....williamsport, pa.

aumick, gertrude l. ....gert ....troy, pa.

austin, ida z. ....peck ....leolyn, pa.

austin, velma m. ....vi ....williamsport, pa.

babyok, mary l. ....smiles ....bentleyville, pa.

baer, iris a. ....ikie ....shickshinny, pa.

baer, ruth d. ....shick ....shickshinny, pa.

bailey, martha e. ....mart ....jersey short, pa.

baker, myrtle e. ....myrt ....marchand, pa.

baker, sophia j. ....bobbie ....simpson, pa.

bardo, marguerite c. ....peg ....muncy, pa.

beebe, virginia r. ....gin ....austin, pa.

bewir, leona a. ....bu ....lawrenceville, pa.

benson, thelma e. ....benny ....susquehanna, pa.

biglin, laretta p. ....biglin ....jermyn, pa.

biglin, mary l. ....lou ....jessup, pa.

bichard, gladys l. ....bich ....montrose, pa.

bowen, virginia ....viv ....geneva, n. y.

boyd, doris j. ....dodie ....coudersport, pa.

boyle, mary ....boyle ....nanticoke, pa.

bridge, mary j. ....bridgie ....susquehanna, pa.

brion, gladys a. ....glad ....liberty, pa.

brion, bernice m. ....bee ....liberty, pa.

brooks, helen l. ....buttercup ....galeton, pa.

brown, eva a. ....brownie ....monroeton, pa.

brown, hazel e. ....brownie ....knoxville, pa.

brown, margaret b. ....peg ....mehoopany, pa.

burley, esther s. ....essie ....west burlington, pa.

bush, alice l. ....peg ....springville, pa.

carr, clarissa m. ....kripsy ....sayre, pa.

carter, h. pauline ....polly ....west auburn, pa.

champney, nellie w. ....bobbie ....gaines, pa.

champney, wilma c. ....billie .... gaines, pa.

chilcott, grace n. ....chilly .... kane, pa.

clark, blanche l. ....bob .... sabinsville, pa.

cleveland, hilda b. ....hil .... mansfield, pa.

comfort, ada l. ....peddy ....troy, pa.

cooper, elizabeth c. ....peg ....kingston, pa.

coulter, kathryn l. ....kay ....punxsutawney, pa.

crispwell, leth l. ....crispy ....noxen, pa.

cronk, beatrice ....bee .... towanda, pa.

cummings, lillian s. ....lill ....mansfield, pa.

curtiss, marion ....curt ....mansfield, pa.

darrow, edith b. ....e. d. ....montrose, pa.

davis, i. arline ....jr. ....meadville, pa.

davis, marjorie ....marg ....middlebury, pa.

derr, dora g. .... d ....hughesville, pa.

ditchburn, mary e. ....madie ....arnot, pa.

dobbie, eleanor t. ....dobbie ....scranton, pa.

dougherty, margaret t. ....peg ....middletown, n. y.

downin, louise t. ....weezie ....harrisburg, pa.

du bert, marion a. ....peggy ....milan, pa.

dull, edith p. ....puss ....sugar run, pa.

dunn, marion e. ....dunny ....montgomery, pa.

ellis, ava p. ....avil ....towanda, pa.

evans, bertha s. ....bert ....powell, pa.

deming, hazel l. ....dem ....mansfield, pa.

fletcher, frances f. ....fanny ....herrick center, pa.

flood, jane i. ....jennie ....sayre, pa.

ford, winifred p. ....winnie ....covington, pa.

fox, m. alice ....al ....wyalusing, pa.

franke, r. harold ....frankie ....blossburg, pa.

french. bernice d. ....frenchy ....elmira, n. y.

frey, elizabeth r. ....betty ....wilkes-barre, pa.

friends, irene m. ....renie ....mansfield, pa.

fuller, verna e. ....dusty ....mansfield, pa.

gay, gladys e. ....gladie ....towanda, pa.

geist, lillian l. ....geist ....chinchilla, pa.

gernert, lillian l. ....lillie ann....columbia x roads, pa.

gilbridi, helen a. ....gilbie ....moosic, pa.

giles, verna m. ....hepsi ....jermyn, pa.

graham, gladys l. ....glad ....tioga, pa.

greeley, thelma ....thel ....westfield, pa.

hanns, regina m. ....genie ....moosic, pa.

hart, martha m. .... mart...................morris, pa.

haverly, hazel r. ....hazie ....sayre, pa.

henning, h. ruth ....shorty ....kane, pa.

hibbard, elizabeth l. ....betty ....elmira, n. y.

hickox, marrian ....hick ....gibson, pa.

hite, r. elizabeth ....betty ....wyalusing, pa.

hiznay, irene d. ....winnie ....jessup, pa.

hoffman, erma ....hoffy ....montgomery, pa.

hoffman, martha d. ....mart ....montgomery, pa.

holcomb, olive b. ....ollie .... leroy, pa.

hopfer, frances f. ....hoppie ....dalton, pa.

hoppe, esther l. ....ikie ....nicholson, pa.

hoppe, mary i. ....buddy ....nicholson, pa.

hugh, louise a. ....weesie ....tioga, pa.

hurd, helen e. ....hurd ....lawrenceville, pa.

jacobs, june b. ....jacobs ....elkland, pa.

jacobson, lerene t. ....curley ....arnot, pa.

james, dorothea m. ....dot ....coudersport, pa.

james, marguerite e. ....peggy ....coudersport, pa.

jankiewicz, julia c. ....jule ....wilkes-barre, pa.

jerald, louise d. ....weezie ....mansfield, pa.

johnson, elizabeth d. ....betty ....laceyville, pa.

judge, mary d. ....tillie ....pittston, pa.

kane, helen i. ....kanie ....susquehanna, pa.

keib, m. louise ....ki ....genesee, pa.

kelly, ann m. ....,.........kelly ....archbold, pa.

kelly, margaret m. ....peg ....susquehanna, pa.

kelts, harriett e. ....harry ....knoxville, pa.

kemp, lina e. ....lin ....shinglehouse, pa.

kennedy, frances l. ....kennedy ....olyphant, pa.

kibbe, f. vivian ....viv ....genesee, pa.

knapp, alice a. ....al ....sayre, pa.

kohler, mildred m. ....mil ....honesdale, pa.

lee, hazel i. ....chicky ....center moreland, pa.

lilley, marian e. ....lil ....new albany, pa.

linberger, catherine l. ....cathie ....elmira heights. n. y.

lippert, dorothy e. ....dot ....honesdale, pa.

mcdonald, beatrice m. ....bea ....goshen, n. y.

mc inroy, eunice m. ....eunice ....middlebury, pa.

mac morran, f. irene ....mickey ....towanda, pa.

mang, marian a. ....petite ....honesdale, pa.

mapes, harriet a. ....harry ....wyalusing, pa.

masters, irene r. ....sunshine ....old forge, pa.

maynard, muriel ....mur ....nanticoke, pa.

mitchell, e. lucille ....luke ....tioga, pa.

molyneaux, grace a. ....gracious ....forksville, pa.

monley, mildred a. ....mil ....jessup, pa.

morre, alice l. ....al ....jersey mills, pa.

morris, grace m. ....gracious ....blossburg, pa.

morrow, marian e. ....mikey ....towanda, pa.

mudge, larena l. ....mudge ....mansfield, pa.

newhard, mary catherine ....kate ....montgomery, pa.

norton, walter, l. ....walt ....hillsgrove, pa.

nunn, m. marie ....kitty ....muncy, pa.

oehrli, ernestine a. ....teeney ....williamsport, pa.

o'herron, helen m. ....blondie ....arnot, pa.

parker, anor d. ....norry ....elmira, n. y.

parks, dorothy l. ....dot ....elmira, n. y.

passmore, vivian m. ....viv ....blossburg, pa.

pearce, e. irene ....tillie ....kylertown, pa.

pettes, virginia l. ....ginger .... orwell, pa.

pizer, kathryn l. ....,.......kay ....jermyn, pa.

precit, stella m. ....tod ....mansfield, pa.

randell, lyndell b. ....lyn ....,......attleboro, mass.

rees, elizabeth e. ....bettie .... costello, pa.

renville, helen b. ....ren ....susquehanna, pa.

reynolds, ruth r. ....ruthie ....whitesville, n. y.

ruggles, eloise f. ....rug ....mainesburg, pa.

rumsey, b. leon ....leo ....mansfield, pa.

rumsey, marian e. ....boots ....gillett, pa.

ryan, catherine m. ....kay ....susquehanna, pa.

ryan, mary i. ....curly ....lawrenceville, pa.

sanguiliano, marie f. ....mer ....wilkes-barre, pa.

sealy, doris l. ....boots ....taylor, pa.

sedor, mary j. .... gay ....simpson, pa.

shaw, ruth i. ....perky ....lawrenceville, pa.

sieminski, isabella ....belle ....kingston, pa.

skuse, g. hildreth ....hil ....monroe, n. y.

slivka, anna ....sally ....jessup, pa.

speer, myrtle a. ....speerie ....corning, n. y.

spoor, lois c. ....lou ....susquehanna, pa.

stilwell, marie t. ....ree ....roulette, pa.

story, marian m. ....story ....tunkhannock, pa.

sulkin, minna g. ....min ....northampton, pa.

swatsler, theda-mae ....teed ....smethport, pa.

treat, mary e. ....treats ....mansfield, pa.

van schick, pauline e. ....vanie ....athens, pa.

voinski, sophia a. ....pope ....simpson, pa.

walsh, catherine m. ....kay ....pittstown, pa.

west, dorothy m. ....dot ....middlebury centre, pa.

withka, stella e. ....trix ....simpson, pa.

wood, beatrice murtilla ....bea ....mansfield, pa.

wright, althea m. ....thump ....springfield, pa.

Music Supervisors

anders, mae g.	bubbles	simpson, pa.
austin, raymond d.	ray	mansfield, pa.
barnes, gertrude a.	barnsey	towanda, pa.
beaver, vera a.	ver	troy, pa.
bush, mary l.	bushy	standing stone, pa.
campbell, ann c.	shorty	athens, pa.
coble, thelma	tholm	wellsboro, pa.
crain, margaret l.	peg	east aurora, n. y.
crist, glenwood j.	crist	muncy, pa.
dawe, arthur c.	art	ashley, pa.
edwards, helen l.	ed	wellsboro, pa.
fischler, louise f.	lou	wellsboro, pa.
fischler, margaret f.	migs	wellsboro, pa.
gotwals, david c.	stub	harrisburg, pa.
hoffman, ruth e.	ritz	doylestown, pa.
iorio, frank f.	10-r-10	harrisburg, pa.
karl, mildred m.	milly	allegany, n. y.
langton, louise a.	sally	stevensville, pa.
lloyd, gordon w.	tom	wellsboro, pa.
mc clain, beatrice e.	bea	st. thomas, pa.
mc cord, willitt	bill	harrisburg, pa.
marsh, howard l.	swampy	galeton, pa.
martin, ruth m.	rufus	lancaster, pa.
mellinger, lrene w.	rene	akron, pa.
millis, c. maxine	max	bolivar, n. y.
milnes, maud	maud	rushville, pa.
nelson, elaine m.	nel	sheffield, pa.
oldfield, willis p.	willie	bath, n. y.
olmstead, rosalie	rosy	painted post,, n. y.
sheils, frances m.	fran	towanda, pa.
simpson, alma n.	al	punxsutawney, pa.
smith, alice r.	al	wellsboro, pa.
spear, hilda e.	hildie	chambersburg, pa.

walley, muriel r. ....mur ....allegany, n. y.

wilcox, marjorie ....marg ....wellsboro, pa.

williams, mabel d. ....billie ....uniondale, pa.

woodard, e. merle ....trudy ....mansfield, pa.

wray, lillie m. ....pal ....williamsport, pa.

Home Economics

barcroft, harriet g. ....hatts ....york, pa.

bartholomew, frances e. ....feb ....mansfield, pa.

bond, gertrude a. ....gert ....shickshinny, pa.

bott, esther e. ....es ....nanticoke, pa.

covey, elizabeth a. ....betty ....coudersport, pa.

cummings, margaret l. ....peg ....attleboro, mass.

elliott, gertrude e. ....gertie ....corning, n. y.

franc, ruth n. ....ruthie ....lake ariel, pa.

gilbert, pauline l. ....bete ....knoxville, pa.

gill, helen h. ....jill ....meadville, pa.

green, betty b. ....red ....wellsboro, pa.

grissinger, louise m. ....frenchie ....retreat, pa.

landon, leah f. ....grasshopper ....canton, pa.

lyter, lillian ....lill ....montoursville, pa.

maher, mary p. ....maher ....hopbottom, pa.

maneval, ethel l. ....manie ....liberty, pa.

miller, florence e. ....flo ....liberty, pa.

miller, margaret a. ....peg ....altoona, pa.

parks, margaret e. ....peg ....benton, pa.

shirey, eleanore d. ....irish ....williamsport, pa.

thompson, sare jane ....janie ....harrisburg, pa.

van dervoort, fannie l. ....hanny ....lake ariel, pa.

zimmerman, violet m. ....zim ....pottsville, pa.

Athletics

Football

| E. C. Russell | J. F. Whitmer | Fred Jupenlaz |
| Coach | Assistant Coach | Trainer |

Football

EVIEWING THE PAST SEASON with an eye to tolerance, conditions and materials, we can easily say with all earnestness that the boys made it a complete success. Five victories, one loss and one tie, allow any aggregation of bruising gridders to hold their brows high in any company. If statistics could be used, Mansfield would have a perfect season, because if you read the games in terms of territory gained and first downs, our up-state team was never outplayed. Coach Russell and his colleagues can certainly feel proud of the showing. The five long scores in the Mountaineers column speak for themselves in the write-ups. The tie game, with all due respect to the Goddess of Breaks, should have been Mansfield's without shadow of doubt. The loss was no disgrace, since two of our worthy backfield crossed the line to the Promised Land, and were called back by doubtful technicalities. We say doubtful because a man's shoe can hardly be big enough to step outside when he is four yards away from said line. Still we are good losers and each spectator, player and coach can say with one accord, "Either team could have won the game and boasted accordingly."

We were slightly unfortunate in acquiring injuries with sickening regularity. The list of casualties in practice far exceeded the breaks and bruises of actual warfare. It was at the time of the deadly rivalry of the Bloomsburg tilt, when Miss Fortune stroked the backfield and line the wrong way and eliminated our threat.

In the line we will see no more: Obelkevich, Urban, Mudge, Harkness, Burr, Allis, and Gavitt. Robbed by graduation, the backfield bids adieu to Hill.

| *Harry Scholl* | *Earl Mudge* | *Walter Urban* |
| *Guard, Captain-elect* | *Guard* | *Utility* |

Mansfield 20
Clarion 0

A distinguishing feature of the first game of the season lay in the comparison of downs. Twenty first downs for the Red and Blacks against zero for Clarion. Ragged playing was the dish served up on both teams, yet despite the Mountaineers' attempts to help Clarion, the aid was refused and in some way Mansfield came out on top. A large influx of material partly aided Mansfield's confusion, since the Coach had many green men whom he wanted to put under fire. A wise move, this wholesale substituting, which later in the season proved invaluable. "Horse" Earle Mudge loomed like a squat giant at guard, stopping everything in his area and slowing up all other plays in a wide swathe. Frank Simms slashed through right tackle, causing deadly damage.

CAPTAIN OBELKEVICH

His swan song finished, good old "Hank" will wend his way to deeds that will encompass and surpass our opinion, formed upon the foundation of four years' action. This we hope.

Henry, as he was christened, was intended by nature to be other than a football player. He was designed for something big and became a football star by accident. Hence he still has his innings coming up.

Indomitable will exercised over an average body, gave that body a hardness of steel, which carried this individual "Hank" through battles where others wilt.

Carlton Harkness	*Howard Burr*	*Mark White*
End	*End*	*Half-back*

Mansfield 40
Susquehanna 0

Everything in the football menu worked to perfection in this game, with the exception of the aerial attack. Five heaves through the ozone nosed the turf for no gains. "Chuck" Hartman, diminutive speed king, burned up the turf in sensational style, gaining on every play with an average of fifteen yards. The half-time score gave Mansfield the edge 7-0, but that second period, woof. Mansfield seemed to have been held back and then severed loose. Susquehanna had the ball in Mountaineer territory once during the entire scrap. That lone exception resulted from a fumble. Mansfield garnered twenty-one first downs vs. none for the visitors. Harry Scholl brightened his star with his stone-wall defense at right guard.

Ellsworth Allis	William Gilvary	Howard Baker
Full-back	*End*	*Half-back*

Mansfield 6
Lock Haven o

Expecting a tough game at Lock Haven, we got it. But not because Lock Haven was too tough an aggregation. Merely through the use of "Old Man Bungle", did the Red and Blacks almost give Lock Haven the session. Lock Haven's lone chance to score came in the third quarter with the ball on the two-yard line and four downs to try. Right there Mansfield's line worked like a clock and the ball was driven far out of danger by Baker's trusty boot. Baker and Webster, two new backs, furnished the fireworks in the backfield, while Pish ran the ends with smashing power. Penalties were Lock Haven's biggest ground gainers, Mansfield giving up eighty-five yards by gift of the referee.

| Frank Simms | Michael Hrycenko | Martin Pish |
| Tackle | End | Half-back |

Mansfield 0
Cortland 0

This struggle can be classed with the answer to the riddle of the sphinx. Mansfield outrushed, outplayed, and outclassed Cortland from start to finish, gaining nineteen first downs against two for Cortland. Weakness in forward passing lost several touchdowns and seventy yards in penalties lost the rest. Mansfield wore the welcome out on Cortland's doorstep and still came only close. Ellsworth Allis, at full, plunged through the Cortland line at will, having an average of five yards for every time he carried the ball. Gilvary gathered in two one-hand grabs at a flying pigskin, which was a sight for sore eyes. Bill received an injury in the fourth quarter which placed him on the shelf for the season.

Edward Hill
Quarterback

Lester Squier
Tackle

Walter Webster
Full-back

Mansfield 7
Oswego 6

The goal line felt alien footsteps for the first time during the season and Mansfield bumped into unexpected opposition and the first hard test of the schedule. Oswego brought a real aggregation to our grid and supplied innumerable exciting moments with threat after threat. Oswego scored on a long pass, and two line smashes in the second quarter and lost the game by failure to make good the try-for-point. White having scored in the first quarter for Mansfield on straight football and Baker having kicked the point. "Heinie" stood out like a beacon in this game with his terrific smashes at the line. Oswego was advancing swiftly up the field as the gun fired.

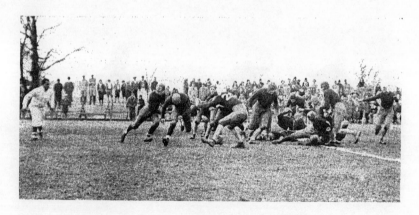

Jarius Gavitt   Charles Hartman   Gordon Lloyd
Tackle   Half-back   Quarterback

Mansfield 0
Bloomsburg 12

Here we have the irresistible force meeting the immovable object, and besides losing to Bloomsburg, the goal was crossed twice more. We caught Bloomsburg at the peak of her form, while we were forced to play with a team of cripples. Hartman scored on an end run, but the head linesman ruled him out of bounds on the twenty-yard line. From that point on Mansfield weakened rapidly and gave Bloomsburg her much needed chances to rip through to score. The entire game proved to be a duel of aerial tosses and although Mansfield more than held up her end of passes completed and yards gained, they unfortunately were not in scoring territory. Burr and Harkness starred on the ends.

Leo Allis
Center

Ned Haynes
Manager

Lloyd Straughn
Utility Center

Mansfield 53
Ithaca 0

Ithaca Physical Ed. College had the honor of taking the worst beating of the season from Mansfield. In this fracas Mansfield put upon the field the entire squad, including every man who had been out for football during the season. Hrycenko, E. Allis, and Hartman, each scored a touchdown, while White and Baker scored two each. Every department of the game worked to perfection for Mansfield and the College went into mourning because it was a week too late. To rub it in Ithaca did not get a first down.

During the season Mansfield scored 125 points to opponents 18. The Red and Black Mountaineers who have played their last as stars are: Hill, L. Allis, Straughn, Mudge, Harkness, Burr, Captain Obelkevitch, Gavitt and Urban.

Basketball

Kimble Marvin
Couch

Edgar Frear
Manager

Kenneth Dayton
Assistant Manager

Basketball

ANSFIELD BY VIRTUE OF STATE AUTHORITY has topped the State basketball world twice in the last four years. Facing the stiffest schedule she ever had, indecision played hand in hand with budding determination, and throughout three games we could not tell whether we had a championship outfit or not. But the fourth game gave the mountaineers all the confidence that a top-notch team needs, and we sailed through the rest of the schedule with some close squeaks, but all wins. An undefeated season in stiff college competition is so rare that we can hardly be blamed for crying to the skies about our own beloved, yes, admirable bunch of boys we know so well.

It is not every team that can take eleven games in succession and still be going strong when the season ends, but such is the story this year. Perhaps one would be led to believe that Mansfield had all the breaks because of two victories by a one-point margin, but anyone who saw the boys in action can say without hesitation that the Mountaineers were not outplayed during the enire season. Bloomsburg and Westchester furnished the stiffest opposition, but each of them bowed to Mansfield on their own court. Dickinson, who had taken over Mansfield on two previous years, were humbled twice this season. Allis, Kelly, Brace, Miller, Augustine and Weeks carried the greatest share of the playing load, but the ability of the utility men to come through in the pinches is what made the outfit effective Unlike some former years there was no star.

Coach Marvin in the condensed opinion of all the students wears the halo of glory, which surrounds a man who has his system and proves that it works better than the rest. He has worked, slaved and molded his own ways into a form that was easily acquired by the men under his wing and in doing so he did not neglect to build material for the years to come. In truth, we too often neglect to offer the praise to fit the accomplishment.

We lose our great combination, much to our sorrow, this year. The Champs who say so-long are: Allis, Kelly, Brace, Miller, Augustine, and Straughn.

Harold Brace
Forward

Paul Miller
Center

Francis Kelly
Guard

Mansfield, 31   *Scranton Business College, 20*

The opener against Scranton didn't prove anything except that we had a team to put on the floor that would make trouble for the coming opponents. Brace, Miller, Kelly, Allis, all four-year basketball men, made the conventional line-up, with Weeks added as the extra man. All the substitutes saw action, and while Scranton looked dangerous at times, they looked equally dizzy in the interims. They were passed to death. Miller scored fourteen points and Brace ten.

Mansfield, 54   *Lock Haven, 14*

Victim Number Two, Lock Haven by name, took a terrific beating, despite the advanced dope to the effect of having a formidable line-up. Lock Haven never really realized just what happened that night. It was, in short, a nightmare of Mountaineer balls swishing through the loop, and but for the numerous substitutions, the score would have reached dizzy heights. Every man on the squad scored points, with Brace leading the van by twelve. In the first half Lock Haven got one field goal.

CAPTAIN ALLIS

"Leo" falls into the heading of great leaders. He has first, the knowledge of the game he plays down to a science. He has second, the ability to accompany that knowledge. He has third, the splendid body to accompany the other two, and he has fourth, the personality to encompass them all. A captain, after all, is necessarily a man who can always show the way to his fellows, and keep his place despite all opposition through sheer worth. In Leo we lose a machine of steel, run by a mind of high intelligence and governed by kingly sportsmanship.

149

Mansfield, 38   Stroudsburg, 24

In the first real test of the season, the Mountaineers assayed all gold. Stroudsburg had never been beaten by Mansfield cagers, and the subsequent victory gave the Red and Blacks all the courage and fight in the world. It would take pages of description to tell of the game, yet Stroudsburg's speed and skill were surpassed by far when the Mountaineers whirled into action. Augustine, Miller, Brace and Kelly all scored heavily, with Allis guarding as though his life was in the balance.

Mansfield, 24   Dickinson, 20

Dickinson sprang a surprise by putting up a far better game than advance reports specified. Mansfield again passed to perfection, but the eagle eyes were slightly off-color, and the only thing that saved the unmarred record was the never-say-die spirit. The Montaineers had that and then some. Augustine leaped to the fore with remarkable ability, with Miller and Brace giving perfect aid. Four straight.

Mansfield, 43   Lock Haven, 18

New combinations occupied the menu for the night at Lock Haven and all of the subs on both the second and third teams saw bits of battle. That gave Lock Haven a chance to lift their usual score to eighteen. Miller scored seventeen points in almost as many minutes, and if he had not been removed would have reached a hundred. All first five men went like the proverbial house on fire. Number five.

Mansfield, 36   Bucknell Frosh, 22

Augustine again stepped to the fore and took all the glare off Bucknell's nice, new, shiny Frosh outfit by dropping seventeen counters through the loop. Bucknell's principal exhibit was Chenowith, who counted ten points for his Alma Mater. Mansfield's attack riddled the visiting team's five-man defense full of holes, and with superb playing beat one of the best Frosh outfits in the country.

Mansfield, 41   Bloomsburg, 40

The seventh straight win came very nearly being the one that broke the camel's back. Such a game is conducive of apoplexy, and the tense feeling of the packed gym swayed from the opening whistle to the last shot. Kelly supplied the highlight drama by dropping a long steve with thirty seconds to go, and winning the fracas. Every man on the team again scored high. The Mountaineers now looked like champions.

Leo Allis
Guard

Ferris Lutes
Forward-Center

Lloyd Straughn
Center

Mansfield, 39   Bloomsburg, 24

Bloomsburg returned to our territory the next week loaded for bear, but Mansfield was loaded for lions. Changing the attack from a long shot game back to short passes and sifting defense work, they surprised "Bloom" into submission. The Maroon and Gold fought with all their traditional fierceness and no doubt would have done better but for inner strife on their team. Miller, Allis and Brace starred with a vengeance.

Mansfield, 43   Elizabethtown College, 25

A newcomer on the schedule supplied the ninth victim. Elizabethtown College came as an unknown quantity, but when measured up to Red and Black standards were found wanting. Every man on the squad, twelve in number, got an opportunity to show his wares and he did. In the short period which all players were in, it was hard to pick a star; they were all stars.

Mansfield, 22   West Chester, 21

The State Championship! The goal in sight came with the tenth struggle, as also did the best game in West Chester's career. The hard trip told heavily upon the Mountaineers and it took the game of their lives to bring them out on the long end. Still keeping that keen passing attack they could not seem to locate the hoop. The close score does not tell of the vastly superior class of the Red and Blacks. But the boys came through, despite heavy odds, and carried off the *State Championship* to the Mountains.

Mansfield, 26   Dickinson, 18

Remembering the close call at Dickinson, the Red and Blacks took no chances and started right out with victory in their grasp. It seemed as though they were tantalizing the down-staters in the manner that they pulled away when the going got close. Five men, Augustine, Miller, Brace, Kelly and Allis, doffed their suits in this last game for their Alma Mater. Straughn, first substitute, also wept his last. We bid goodbye to a great combination in these boys. The best we've ever had.

"Pablo"

Baseball

NUCLEUS OF BASEBALL TEAM

Standing: Donald Roderick, Frances Kelly, Michael Hrycenko,
Harry Bartlow, Manager.
Sitting: Angelo Scarcello, Harold Brace, Ed. Hill.

Baseball

W HERE IS THE AMERICAN YOUTH who has not had his dreams of the
horsehide? Who is the oddity of life who has not tried to play some position or all upon a team? Baseball starts with an all-consuming ambition
from the earliest understanding of sport up to the point of bitter realization that he
cannot play ball or to the great moment when he discovers that he can play. From this
junction come the two divisions of a glorious game, the fan and the player.

A baseball fan is the embodiment of the average American. Realizing that it
is impossible for him to become the player of his dreams, he gets behind those who can
play and boosts, ardently, joyously, fervently, and even sinfully. Mr. Fan is just as
important to the good old game as is Mr. Star. Mr. Fan invariably causes Mr. Star to
rise to his greatness or fall to his failure. He is the umpire's idea of Satan; he is the
ball-hawk's idea of criminal souvenir hunters; he is the apex of praise; he is the dregs
of sarcasm or the inflamer of hate; he is all that he should be and all that he shouldn't.
What more could you ask?

The player is schooled in the art of ball tossing, quick thinking, co-ordination
and muscular activity. He sometimes plays for the love of the sport and at other
times plays for what's in it. At all times he is the unknown quantity of the manager's
despair. He is the man for whom cash is paid and emotion is returned.

In years gone by we, as a college, have more than done our share to give to
the national pastime great players, good umpires, inspired managers and fiery,
staunch-souled fans.

The season of 1929 ushers in bright prospects for an unscarred schedule. We have as a nucleus a bunch of the best-looking material that has ever graced that rough-cut diamond on the shores of the Tioga. Taking up the brighter side of the question, the infield we have always praised as the best in college circles, still remains intact. Kelly at third, Hill at short, Pish or Hrycenko at second and Gilvary at first, are a sight for trachoma. The outfield again calls Brace and Scarcello its own and then reserves a spot for some rookies favored by the smile of the Goddess of Fortune. Since pitchers always seem to do some work in a game, Roderick and Weidman have about cinched positions in the early season workouts. Roderick is a veteran of previous wars. Terry and Gilvary are likely-looking prospects for the twirling section. If everything were perfectly rosy, the coach, one Marvin by name, would lose his job, so in order to fix that up, we have run out of catchers. No veterans or men of experience are available for this season. But Krutzeck, Wilkinson, Justin, Summers, and Dunbar are working like beavers for the post.

From this bunch and many other candidates we hope to produce a combination that will do credit to the Alma Mater. If we don't come out on top, it can never be said we haven't tried. A Mansfield team always fights to the last drop.

When this annual is in your hands the baseball season will no doubt be complete and since it is impossible to forecast accurately that part is left to your sight. At an early season writing we know that Mansfield has everything but the championship. Following is the schedule in which you can inscribe your own data. And when the smoke clears away let us hope that the columns will read all wins, no losses.

The schedule:

	M.	O.
April 26, Stroudsburg S. T. C...Here		
May 1, Cortland S. N. S......Away		
May 4, Cortland S. N. S.......Here		
May 8, Bloomsburg S. T. C...Away		
May 11, Bucknell Frosh ....Here		
May 15 Cook Academy ......Away		
May 18, Bloomsburg S. T. C....Here		
May 25, Brockport S. N. S. ....Here		

Kimble Marvin, '16...........Coach
K. F. Van Norman, '06·...Grad. Mgr.
Harry Bartlow, '29..Student Manager
Benn Weeks, '30 ..Business Manager

Minor Sports

Weeks, Cruttenden, Trowbridge, Straughn.

Tennis

A MAN LEARNING TO SWIM has had no greater struggle than tennis at Mansfield has had to gain recognition in the world of sports. For years the exponents of the sport have been trying to introduce tennis as a major brand of ball, and despite the fact that we have had many unattached experts playing merely for the exercise for the last twenty years, it has seemed impossible to band together a team to represent the Alma Mater on the field of battle. Attempts, many-fold, panned out in as many washouts, as far as varsity tennis was concerned and the only lasting influence of the plan lay in the desire to make the idea concrete.

Tennis requires the largest amount of exertion per time of any sport in existence. It is the most beneficial in view of muscle building, co-ordination, sportsmanship and alertness. Truly, it has been called by many, "The sport of the Kings."

We have always had excellent facilities at Mansfield to play the game and these facilities have not been wasted. Faculty members vie with students in producing players who can at any time place with top-notchers. Students participate more largely in tennis than any other game in the college. It can easily be called the sport of the proletariat as well as the sport of kings. Despite this remarkable adaption of the game to the vast number of people it has remained in oblivion insofar as Mansfield's athletics have been concerned. Other colleges have made it a major sport, why not Mansfield?

1928 gave tennis a very good start and the boys on the team added considerably to the impetus by taking over every team they opposed. Among these victms were Bloomsburg, Alfred, Dickinson and Cortland. The group making possible these victories were Lloyd Straughn, Maurice Cruttenden, John Trowbridge and Benn Weeks. All of these men are available for the 1929 team, probably against the same opponents as were lacquered last year.

Girls' Hockey

BITTER COMPETITION REIGNED supreme amongst the girls this thirty-two weeks. The girls traded a right for a right and a left for a left. The Medes and the Persians never fought more fiercely. The Frosh started out to make the upperclassmen look weak and like nobody's business and when Hockey sallied into view it looked as though supremacy of the Sophomore ash-wielders was a thing of the limbos. Hockey is a great game and a torrid one. Many a girls' shin and black-spotted anatomy will testify as to that. A wild swing, indefinite contact, and we have the indirect result and a few miscellaneous burnt-up phrases, which everyone is liable to utter.

It seems as though the girls are very prolific hockey players and therefore are able to get in quite a lot of the little wooden pellet. They go in so much, in fact, it is doubtful whether the Sophs will ever play again. The Frosh won every game except one, that game the Frosh generously served to the Sophs upon a platter.

After the massacre comes the peace which one only finds in the grave. Basketball sent the fever up a little higher and in the first contest the Frosh again triumphed 23-8. But the Sophs must have been under dopy influence because they walloped the Frosh in the next two games so badly that most of the Frosh will probably enter the convent. Beaver, Baumunk, Eldridge, Chamberlain, Smith and Shollenberger supplied the victorious sextet with points. The Frosh sported Bridge, MacDonald, Levitt, Rymkiewicz, Cronk and Reinwald as the team that tried but couldn't come through. So we'll call it a fifty-fifty break for the year.

Intramural Sports

$\mathcal{S}$ TRUGGLING FOR RECOGNITION among the extra-curricular activities of the College, Intramural Sports have been floundering about for four years. Three years ago saw the successful completion of the ideal program in the line of smaller sports. At that time the famed Comets produced a fast squad to cop the pennant. Since then minor athletics have been a questionable topic. But 1929 marked a change in the fortunes of the lesser genus of athletics that was not to be denied, and again somewhat like the Easter crocus, Intramural raised its head.

Fast ball was dished up to the customers from the initial game to the last played, and one of the few regrets was that the league games were unable to be completed, thereby making it a necessity to pick the uncrowned champion upon the point basis.

We take great pleasure in announcing the winner of the 1929 Basketball League of Mansfield State, namely: South Fourth or the Comets II. The Comets had undoubtedly the fastest and cleverest squad of the league and managed to play off the entire schedule, being the only team to accomplish that feat. Wilton Moyer, J. Brit Davis, Glenn Wolfanger, Anthony Cymbal, Mike Hrycenko,, Al Dunbar, Anthony Suhocke and Leigh Bower comprised the squad. High Scoring honors in a single game were acquired by Wilton Moyer, who scored twenty-three points against South Third. Seasonal high scoring honors were tied by Moyer and Brit Davis with fifty-three points apiece. Gilvary, of the N. Fourth team, came third with twenty-nine points. Bill was also one of the stars of the league and played a keen game at his center position throughout the season. Miller and Bartlow, of the Second Floor aggregation, tied for fourth place with twenty-two counters each. White, with twenty points, nosed out his team-mate, Spencer, who had rolled up nineteen. Hrycenko, scoring seventeen points, finished slightly ahead of Wolfanger, who looped in fourteen.

Team scoring for the season is as follows: South Fourth, 180 points in eight games; North Fourth, 80 points in six games; South Third, 62 points in five games; Second, 60 points in five games; North Third, eight games forfeited.

Picking an all-star team from the excellent material within the league is an exceedingly hard job, and picking such aggregations will undoubtedly call forth undue criticism. The first and second teams have been selected for the following reasons: 1. Scoring power. 2. Playing ability. 3. Games played.

First Team		*Second Team*
Moyer—S. Fourth	Forward	Frear—S. Third
Davis—S. Fourth	Forward	Spencer—N. Fourth
Gilvary—N. Fourth	Center	Wolfanger—S. Fourth
Hrycenko—S. Fourth	Guard	White—N. Fourth
Fiske—Second	Guard	Cymbal—S. Fourth
Miller—Second	Alternate	Dunbar—S. Fourth
Bartlow—Second	Alternate	Parkes—S. Third

Historical sidelights are always exceedingly interesting and now we will have a little glimpse into the past and see just what it was that made Old Lady Intramural shorten her tresses and bob her hair, thereby vamping the young bloods into fiery action. 1925 saw little action, with nobody having enough ambition to shoot a few of their own. But we cannot neglect the J. H. S. Faculty, who had a magnificent schedule of two games, of which they lost both to the J. H. S. Varsity, very badly.

1926-27 gave birth to the first organized effort of a league. To this Dean Balch was God-father, dictator, score-keeper, medal awarder, etc. He gave all these things together with the championship to Comets I, the greatest little team in the history of the college. We say little, because the six players comprising the outfit averaged 5 feet ten inches, and scored according to their height.

1927 saw the intramural efforts devolve into the waste basket, due to the class organization which did not hitch. However, if the edge must be given, the Frosh have it.

1928-29, you can easily see, as stated above, Comets II, had the banana oil.

Activities

Administrative

THE STUDENT COUNCILS

Top row, left to right: J. Brit Davis, Dolly Gleokler, Elwood Kendall, Helen Howard, Miriam Howells.

Middle row: Mae Light, Benn Weeks, Clare Sperry, Harry Scholl, Helen Swartz, Julia Beaver.

Lower row: Carleton Harkness, Helen Haight, Howard Burr, President Men's Council; Frances Philp, President Women's Council; Anthony Shelinski, Lydia Rogers.

Student Government

*T*O SAFEGUARD the customs and traditions of Mansfield State Teachers College, to form an executive head for the student body, and to create a closer and more harmonious co-operation between the students and faculty as well as within the circle of the great student family, the Student Council movement was first organized in 1918. From the very beginning this embryo has grown and each year progressed until at last the full-fledged organism has developed into an efficient working body. Its membership embraces eighteen students seven of whom are elected by the men and eleven by the women of the school.

Originally the plan was to have two separate councils, one for the men and one for the women working independently of each other. At this time there were very few downtown students, so it was not necessary to have downtown representatives on the student governing bodies. With the rapid growth of the college the enrollment soon exceeded the dormitory capacity and as a result each year more and more students were forced to lodge in private homes throughout the vicinity. In the spring of 1927 this number had reached such proportions that a real downtown problem of government and co-operation existed. To alleviate this difficulty and to bring all students into a closer proximity, a downtown council was established. This functioned fairly well but did not fulfill expectations—there was still a break—a gap not bridged— between the downtown students and the school activities. After one year's existence this council died a natural death. Another plan was instigated in the spring of 1928 whereby students from the urban district were represented on the regular council by three of their number. This seems to be a much more efficient solution and bids fair to become the precedent for future years. Thus these two councils fused into one—the Women's Council. This leaves the Men's and Women's Councils still working more or less apart, but with the same objectives in view.

Since both councils were working in the same direction, toward the same goal, the deans and the council members decided in 1926 that greater efficiency could be obtained if the two organizations would work in unison; this resulted in a partial consolidation in that the two councils would hold joint meetings and as far as possible handle all business under this one group. This method proved very successful during the first year, coming nearer the desired goal of equilibrium than either council had attained individually. Under this joint system each council maintained its own rule over the respective dormitories and dealt individually with the problems clearly within its own boundaries. However, each group was susceptible to suggestions and aids from the other—thereby making the girls advisors to the men and vice versa. The end of the school term in the spring of 1927 brought a slump in the joint-council program. When school opened the following fall much of the interest and punch had gone out of the inter-council idea and once more the two groups worked separately, meeting in joint session only when problems of common concern commanded the attention of both groups. Individually each council's work was termed a success, although they had not co-operated to the degree necessary to bring about the greatest possible good to the greatest number of students with the least amount of time and energy.

This fact was realized when the councils for '28-'29 were organized, so once more the joint council idea and interest crystallized into a smooth working organization of men and women. Since every organization has some purpose for which it exists, the student councils must not be an exception. These two governing bodies exist for service —service to the students of the college—to the faculty—and ultimately to every local- ity where a Mansfield student may go. This service may be likened unto a great octopus, each tentacle a definite branch of service, reaching out into all phases of college life. The purpose of each council is that of serving as a representative group of the student body, exercising student supervision over all student affairs outside of organized athletics, fostering Mansfield traditions and customs, acting as an inter- mediary between students and the faculty and administering and playing an important part in handling all cases of infraction of College rules.

The '28-'29 councils have striven to act always for the best interest of the College. Blessed with a fine Principal, broad-minded Deans and an exceptionally fine group of members, with popular presidents to lead them, the councils feel that they have met and faithfully tried to solve the problem of bettering student life at Mans- field. Each student, each person who has sojourned in the College surroundings, will carry with him certain memories of his college career. These he will wish to per- petuate and hold in the recesses of his mind forever, and it is in the hope of making this possible, together with the hope of increasing the number of pleasant memories, that the councils have endeavored to give their best to their College.

Standing: Howard Burr, Wendell Davis, K. R. Jones, Jr., Prof. George Strait.
Sitting: J. Brit Davis, Benn Weeks, Harry Summers, Donald Roderick.

Y. M. C. A.

THE Y. M. C. A. CABINET

President .... Harry Summers
Vice President........... J. Brit Davis
Secretary.............. K. R. Jones, Jr.
Treasurer........... Howard M. Burr

Devotional Secretary.... Wendell Davis
Deputation Secretary.. Donald Roderick
Social Secretary.......... Benn Weeks
Faculty Sponsor .... George Strait

YOUNG MEN'S CHRISTIAN ASSOCIATION, commonly known as the Y. M. C. A., is one of the greatest and best known of young men's organizations in the country. In every city and nearly every small town and village one sees the "Y" triangle. Mansfield was one of the first Normal Schools to have this organization within the institution. Our club rooms, the "Y" Hut, built several years ago to furnish a place for the fellows to spend their leisure time in, serves its purpose admirably. It is a pleasure that home and the "Y" hut alone may furnish, to go there during the cold winter days and sit before the open fireplace to read or talk or play the piano and victrola. It is a place where the new students get acquainted with the best in the school. In this way it is the "big brother" to all Freshmen. Everything possible entertainment is there.

The "Y" acts as a spiritual agency to start the young man on the right track in his school career. The weekly devotional services are planned to appeal to the fellows. Many out-of-town speakers, as well as prominent down-town men and faculty members give talks that are greatly enjoyed by those who like to hear something worthwhile. The organization has access to the best musical talent in the school for

168

these devotional services. The spiritual side of the student's life is not the only one considered, because the "Y" has its annual hike, dance, and pool and checker tournaments. All members are urged to participate in all these affairs. As a social center the hut is second to no place. The boys meet there and use it as a recreation room. The spacious porch is literally packed with young men during the warm months of the school year.

The "Y" does not confine its benefits to school members, but has a Gospel Team which is more than glad to conduct services in any church in the vicinity. So the work of the "Y" is felt generally.

The Gospel Team

*T*HE GOSPEL TEAM is a representative organization of the Y. M. C. A. at Mansfield. Its purposes are: to be of service to needful churches and communities, to help spread Christianity; to stimulate a genuine Christian spirit and character; and broaden the influence of the Y. M. C. A. The one chief aim of the Gospel Team is service. It is always willing and ready to assist any needing community.

This team is a little different from the athletic teams of the school but it functions somewhat in the same way. The President of the "Y" calls for candidates and the men respond. Preparation begins immediately and while the team is preparing a schedule is arranged. After sufficient practice and preparation the team engages in their games. In the history of this organization it has never been known to meet defeat. This record alone stamps it as an outstanding organization of the school.

When the team arrives at the field it is given complete charge of the service. The form of service is simple and is carried on with due reverence and sincerity. The members are not veterans in this sort of work but they are successful because of the spirit with which they enter their job. Each one does his separate work well and naturally this results in a well finished work by the team as a whole.

The benefits of the organization are two in number. Communities are benefitted for they see the young people's point of view of Christianity and every man who is on the team reaps both spiritual and moral benefits as well as fine training.

Members of the year's team are:

Speakers: William Norton, Ed. Tuton, Wendell Davis.

Musicians: Frank Miller, trumpet; Leonard Smith, trumpet; Waldo Seamans, vocal; Donald Roderick, song director; Harry Summers, pianist.

Y. W. C. A. CABINET

Standing: Biesecker, E. Scal, Chamberlain, Wedge, M. Scal, Seagers, Davis.
Sitting: Jarvis, M. Jupenlaz, H. Jupenlaz, Washburn, Pantall.

Y. W. C. A.

Sponsor..............Helen R. Jupenlaz
President..........Madeline Washburn
Vice President.......Matilda Jupenlaz
Secretary.................Mildred Seal
Treasurer............Elizabeth Jarvis

*P*ROBABLY IT IS unnecessary to explain the meaning of the Y. W. C. A. here at Mansfield. College life, as everyone knows, is a very busy one. We have much fun and frolic along with our common interests of the class room but above all this there is something ever greater; something deeper, something quieter, something infinitely more compelling in its power and influence. It enters lives and makes each one purer, broader and more splendid. It is the Christian Spirit which has entered our hearts through the Y. W. C. A. at Mansfield. Among our money raising schemes was the sale of candy, sandwiches and ice cream. We are justly proud of the new furniture, curtains and draperies which were realized from the profits of our schemes. We have also sent funds to Korea and Kentucky which are used in aiding a worthy cause. We are glad of this Y. W. C. A. and the influence it has had in our lives. More than that we are glad for the Christ who is the friend of the school girl. May each girl as she leaves our Alma Mater know better the meaning of this great friendship, live nearer to her God and strive to make her life what He would have it, because of her contact with the Young Women's Christian Association at Mansfield.

Y. W. C. A. Rooms

HE "Y" ROOMS are an addition to North Hall which all girls have enjoyed this year more than ever before. The organization has done much in furnishing it to make it more homelike, attractive and comfortable. Now solid enjoyment and rest await any girl who wishes to go there, if only for a few minutes to sit on the davenport, or in the easy chairs and listen to the radio. These rooms have become a social center for all girls. All students were privileged to use the radio and hear President Hoover's inaugural address. Clubs have social and business meetings in these rooms. To show their appreciation they have given the "Y" books, magazines and desk lamps which all of the girls enjoy using. Very often the girls assemble there at nine o'clock for "Y" song service or parties.

Very attractive teas have been given during the year. The first was given by the "Y" for the purpose of welcoming old students and becoming acquainted with new ones. The Student Council gave a delightful tea and the Frosh a most attractive Spanish Tea for the "big sisters" as a token of appreciation for favors shown them during the year. The "Y" rooms looked very nice clad in Spanish shawls. Student recitals have been given by pupils of Misses Atwater, Perkins and Hartman.

The porch with its new gliders and carpets makes one of the most restful and cooling spots on the campus. From here the campus looks like a huge green carpet with its terraces built as stairs. Beyond the campus one may get a fine view of the town with its many churches and high school.

THE WEARERS OF THE BLOCK "M"

E. Allis	Harkness	Lutes	Simms
L. Allis	Hartman	Mudge	Squier
Augustine	Haynes	Miller	Straughn
Baker	Hill	Obelkevich	Urban
Brace	Hrycenko	Pish	Webster
Burr	Jupenlaz	Roderick	Weeks
Davis	Kelly	Scarcello	Whitmer
Gavitt	Lloyd	Scholl	White
Gilvary			

T HE "M" CLUB was organized years ago under Coach Jones. Its purpose is to promote good fellowship, high scholastic standing, clean sportsmanship, and the idea that it is better to have played one's best and lost than to win under any condition. Mansfield State has had an honorable name in athletics that is greatly to be envied. Not only have the Mansfield teams been consistent winners, but they have been good losers. Visiting teams are always glad to play at our institution.

There are few honors that can be compared to wearing a varsity "M" and so there is no society so exclusive as the "M" Club. To become a member the candidate must have been awarded a letter by the college, take an oath to uphold the purposes and ideals of the college and the club, then undergo the initiation. The initiation is notoriously the toughest in the school. The candidates are subjected to a two-day public initiation and then—then comes the big night when they are tortured into good standing.

The "M" Club has always been popular because of the big open dance which the members give to the rest of the school. Besides this there is in the spring the closed dance to which the "conquering heroes" take their fair damsels for an evening of dancing and entertainment. So it is no wonder that as spring draws near the social athletes take a back seat to the men of the grid or court or diamond.

It is the "M" Club's aim to serve the school and in doing this they help by enforcing the freshmen custom of allowing no letters but "M" to be worn at Mansfield. By helping to promote true school spirit, and by giving their best that Mansfield students may be proud of their Alma Mater in athletics.

Departmental

Home Economics

HOME ECONOMICS is the oldest and greatest profession in the world. Mansfield State Teachers College aims to make the girls who are studying Home Economics efficient and intelligent home makers as well as well-trained teachers. The students electing this course spend four years at Mansfield, at the end of which time, providing they have satisfactorily completed the course of study, they are awarded the degree of Bachelor of Science in Home Economics. They study those subjects which are closely related to life in the home and community, such as foods, clothing, nutrition, textiles, applied art, costume design, millinery, child development, home nursing, and home management. In order to give them a more general education, and to broaden their outlook they take courses in science, art, English, psychology, education, economics, and history.

Much practical work is included in the Home Economics program. Clothing courses include work in construction with opportunity for class criticism, judgment and comparison with ready-to-wear garments. Emphasis is placed upon the selective phase of clothing. Detailed studies are made of food values, and dietaries are planned which meet the food requirements of the various incomes. During their junior year at Mansfield, the Home Economics girls live in a family group in the Home Management House. There they get actual experience in home management which includes marketing, budgeting, selection and care of equipment, interior decorating, as well as meal planning, preparation and serving. During their junior year they also have practical experience in managing a school lunch cafeteria.

The Home Economics course at Mansfield trains teachers of Home Economics, so the students devote part of their junior year to teaching foods, clothing and related activities in the Junior High School at Mansfield. In their senior year they spend six weeks teaching in some vocational high school in the state, under the supervision of Miss Lu M. Hartman, Director of the Department of Home Economics at Mansfield. Thus girls who are graduated from this department are qualified to teach vocational or general home economics in the public schools of Pennsylvania.

Domicilian Club

Vice President..........Nellie Carlson   Secretary.............Frances Hoover
President..........Rosanna Bloomster   Treasurer...............Helen Swartz
Faculty Advisor....Miss Sadie M. Smith

*T*HE VARIOUS CLUBS and organizations in the school make possible the association of like individuals into groups having common purposes and ideals and sponsoring similar projects. They offer the students a congenial medium of expression on an extremely wide range of diverse subjects as well as give them an ample opportunity to exercise, and cultivate, any special talent with which they may be gifted. And so it is with the Domicilian Club. All Home Economic students are eligible for membership. The club has developed and grown with the parent department and become an essential part of every Home Economics girl's life at Mansfield. The Domicilian Club aims to develop comradeship, to promote social life among the girls of the Home Economics Department, and to develop personality, leadership and initiative. This aim is carried out through the varied club programs in which every girl has an opportunity to take an active part int he club work.

But the club activities are not all work. Periodically throughout the year occur "feeds" and amusement programs which require work in the planning and executing, yet meaning to the members a multitude of pleasant times and memories. To the girls, these social functions represent hours of recreation and diversion from the monotony of school routine. They bring excitement and the happy joy in associating with class-mates and friends interested in the same field of endeavor; they denote a healthy atmosphere of comradeship and to every girl of the club they represent an essential and exceedingly happy part of her undergraduate days.

Through these aims and activities the Domicilian Club is justified in maintaining its place among the leading clubs and organizations of the school. May her daughters hold high the crown of womanhood and honor her in the happiness of homes and the large usefulness of purposeful lives.

HOME ECONOMICS SENIORS

Standing: Francis Philp, Ruth Huthmaker.
Sitting: Darthy Thomas, Agnes Persons, Bernice Decker.

HOME ECONOMICS COTTAGE

Training School

O GIVE THOSE who have elected to teach in the first six grades an opportunity to perfect their teaching technique a training school was was built at the north of the campus where the work of the first six grades is done. These first six years of a child's life are important for the establishing of right habits of work and of right feeling, thinking and acting in life situations. During these early years the school attempts to give practice for these individual and social characteristics which distinguish a person of education from mere training. In doing this the student teacher is given her chance, through observation and participation, to learn methods, material and technique in the art of teaching. From the first the school attempts to put both the pupil and student teacher in situations calling for initiative, self-confidence, self-reliance, self-control, careful judgments and social co-operation. As far as the pupil is concerned, all of these are developed within the ability and development ranges of the children.

The program is very flexible. It calls for subject matter at work in broadening the information and enriching the experiences of the children. It demands that children be participators, doers, and not hearers only.

This participation is begun in the first grade. Here in both play and work, each class is a group, or a class, in which individual rights and community interest exist. The codes for behavior and responsibility built up by the children contain many of the principles of right human relationships. The children here receive practice in evaluating acts and situations with personal rights and the common good in mind. The teacher naturally continues to be guide and counsellor, and the person in final authority whenever such authority is needed.

The children express themselves in original dramatizations, in art, music, handwork, in written and oral language. The special teachers of art, music, industrial arts and household arts work in co-operation with the grade supervisors to the end that the vital activities of the children may be enriched through these effective means of expression.

The usual school subjects—reading, writing, arithmetic, spelling, history, geography—make their demands at the very beginning. In the primary grades children want to read and hear about the Indians, the buffalo, the flowers, and other interesting things and people whose lives and experiences they are living. They want stories to tell and dramatize. They want to write about their experiences, to tell about their pets and friends. In their games, their store, and their numerous building projects they must keep scores, count change, learn coins, estimate values, compute and measure, thereby making learning a pleasure instead of a task.

When the children come to the intermediate grades they already have a rich background of history and geography. They can read with understanding. Can use numbers and can express themselves freely in oral and written form. They are already familiar with art, music and the manual arts, in an elementary way, as means of expression.

The program of the intermediate grades grows naturally out of this information into broader and more complex living as the children's viewpoints extend and their experiences advance. When the pupils leave this department they have developed study habits along with knowledge and skill required for effective work in the Junior High School, and along with it all, student teachers have been prepared to go out into the active field where they may carry on teaching as an efficient profession.

Music Supervisors

MUSIC SUPERVISORS' CLUB

President..............Fred Ringrose   Secretary..............Dolly Gleokler
Vice President ..... Lucille Parsons   Treasurer............Donald Roderick

*T*O THOSE WHO ARE specializing in the field of Music excellent opportunities are offered for training and education, not only in developing personal proficiency, but also in appreciating and understanding both the work of their contemporaries and of old masters. Aside from this specialization, it has been made possible for the entire campus to enjoy finer music, both classical and popular, throughout the year. All of this has come especially through the remarkable development during the past several years and more music truly finds a definite place and serves a real purpose in the life of the students at Mansfield.

MUSIC SENIORS

Willard Ehlers   Fred Ringrose   Boghdan Shlanta
    Frank Yurkewitch   George Palmer

R EADING WITH APPRECIATION and hearing good music with appreciation
are fine arts. Music appreciation is stimulated, and the imagination directed
by active participation in the songs and games of childhood. This type of
music appreciation in our public schools is one of the aims of the Music Supervisors.
Even though the pupils never become great musicians or even players of musical
instruments, their life will be richer and fuller because they have learned to appreciate music; they have "learned to listen" and finally they "listen to learn."

In the field of public school music, through the music teachers the pupils
learn and discover that there is rhythm in verse, in work, and even in play, as well as
in music. They acquire a background and atmosphere for real art music; they learn
of fundamental rhythms and instruments. From the kindergarten up through high
school musical knowledge and participation in each branch of the art of music appreciation is gradually widened. A gradually increased knowledge of folk music, of the
lives and picturesque customs of different peoples, of standard instruments, and of
the boyhood and early lives of great composers all tend to more intelligent listening,
and to a greater and deeper enjoyment and appreciation of fine music and of the
instruments that are used.

In 1926 Mansfield reorganized her music department to meet the requirements of a degree course, changing from a three year course with a music certificate
to a four-year course granting the degree of Bachelor of Science in Public School
Music, at the completion of the course. This entitles the owner to teach Public School
Music in Pennsylvania.

In order to afford a field of sufficient extent to give all the student supervisors a chance to engage in a practical work, Mansfield borough, together with several
outlying school districts, has co-operated to serve as the practice teaching laboratory

for the music department. Aside from the academic content of the course each student must have two years practice teaching, three years orchestra, two years band, four years piano and voice, three years stringed instruments and one and one-half year on wind instruments.

In the fall of 1921 the glee clubs were organized by Mrs. Grace Steadman, who up until the fall of 1928 conducted the Orpheus Glee Club for Men. The Cecelian Glee Club for ladies has been under the direction of Mrs. Margaret Steadman. In the fall of 1928 the two clubs were fused into one organization—the Chorus.

Each day the school is impressed with the genius of Dr. Will George Butler, director of the Student Symphony Orchestra, which plays for chapel exercises. During the past twelve years Dr. Butler has directed this orchestra, giving many fine concerts in school and throughout the surrounding country.

Dr. Butler is by far the most outstanding member of the college music faculty. It is to him we owe our thanks for our school song, "Mansfield, Hail!" This is one of the finest school songs in existence, and has been lauded by scores of outsiders. His compositions are not by any means confined to patriotic or school songs, because he has composed many others, among which "Visions of Oleona" is the most famous. Dr. Butler, himself a graduate of Mansfield, has always been a great worker for the advancement of the college, having taken wider interest in the institution than his position as director of the orchestra and member of the faculty really demanded. It is in recognition of his services to Mansfield that the Carontawan Board dedicated their book to him.

Other music organizations are also under competent direction. The concert band, one of the best in the state, is under the leadership of Mr. John Myers. Mr. Donald Baldwin directs the second band, which is made up principally of supervisors who are studying band instruments. A great deal of credit is due both bands for their loyal support to the athletic activities of the school.

Grand Finale of "Pirates of Penzance."

PIRATES OF PENZANCE
A Scene from the First Act of the Sullivan Opera, Produced in 1928.

The Junior High School

*T*HE JUNIOR HIGH SCHOOL was founded for two purposes—the training
of the pupil and the training of teachers in the Junior High School field. In
carrying out the first purpose Mansfield founded the Junior High School on
the belief that the most important function of the school was to look to the well-
rounded development of the individual, not as an individualist, but as an outstanding,
thinking member of society. Provision for individual differences, therefore, is
essentially a foundation of the school. The second purpose, that of training young
men and women to carry out this important, primary function of the school has
brought about the development of a program to meet the practical needs and specialization of teachers under the direction of competent supervisors.

Probably of first importance, is the school's distinctly human attitude toward all its members. The question in mind at all times is: "How can we so use the
school situation and the materials at hand as to bring out the best possibilities in the
individual, either pupil or student teacher?" The answer to this question may sometimes mean making the path a little smoother; it may mean making the going a little
more difficult. But whatever the policy adopted the purpose remains the same.
The school attempts to know each individual as he or she is. When pupils enter the
school they become individuals in a group small enough for the teacher and supervisor
to make personal daily observations of their personal and social behavior traits, and
yet large enough to offer the challenge for endeavor.

Pupils who have real difficulty in any of the school subjects which furnish
the material for their activities are given instruction in small groups (Opportunity
Classes) so that they may gain both the power and the confidence to go forward. A
decision concerning the plan to adopt with a child of unusual brightness must of
necessity rest upon the permanent best interests of the child and is dealt with accordingly. The problems that of necessity arise in the school community are considered to
be questions of mutual interest to teachers and pupils.

Dramatics

D RAMA, the field of expression of great minds throughout the ages, has become woven with a clear design into the fabric of the modern College. Dramatic organizations flourish and succeed. They offer the student excellent opportunity for self-expression, both in thought and execution as it is known to the modern stage; and more essentially, through their public performances and presentations, they make possible the better enjoyment and understanding of plays and acting of the finer type. It is through these activities that their existence is justified and through which they have attained the prominence and received the recognition as a real part of the student life at Mansfield State.

CLUB OFFICERS

President...............*Harry Bailey*   Secretary-Treasurer.... ...*Mary Howe*
Vice President.......*Anthony Shelinski*

CLUB MEMBERS

Allis, Allene	Howe, Mary Hannah	Painter, Louise
Beach, Harry	Homet, Emerson	Spry, Maxine
Beach, Helen	Hardie, Alexander	Smith, Grace
Bailey, Harry	Howard, Helen	Snyder, Austin
Davis, Wendell	Jenkins, Clifford	Smith, Gould
Downin, Louise	Lee, Hazel	Shelinski, Anthony
Dayton, Kenneth	Morgan, Margaret	Swatsworth, Ellen
Evans, Mima	Marsh, Howard	Thompson, Mary
Ellsworth, Lenalys	Nelson, Elaine	Thomas, Margaret
Gilchrist, Margaret	Nichols, Bess	Thomas, Mamie
Howells, Miriam	Norton, Walter	Wydman, Errold

"It is a beautiful thing to live. Life is a fine art.
It is the supreme consummation of all the arts, the final finish and flower."

Club. This year we register our first expressive joy of living by dishing out to our patrons here and at Wellsboro a tempting bit of seasoning called, "Sauce for the Gosling."

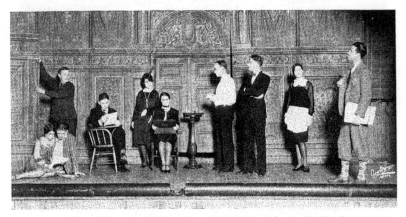

This picture shows us at work preparing "Sauce for the Gosling."

There are about forty of us in our club, or, better perhaps, family. Our purpose in life includes not only the wish to entertain the public, but also the desire to share our talents each with the other. Our family parties take the form of presented programs. An appreciation of the versatility of our members may be gathered from a glance at some of the programs offered:

"The Virginian Judge"—Ellen Swatsworth.
"A War Vet's Reminiscence"—Howard Marsh.
"Betty at the Baseball Game"—Elaine Nelson.
"Tony at the Baseball Game"—Al. Hardy.

The selections were cleverly rendered, and made quite effective through "the art of Myrle Lee," who demonstrated the application of stage "make-up", using these characters for his subjects. At a joint meeting of the Rurban and Dramatic Clubs, there was an expression of friendly hope for a kindred spirit between the clubs. Some clever dramatic ability was revealed in the program, which proved to be a reading, "The King's Daughter," composed and rendered by Myrle Lee, and most effectively interpreted by Fred Ringrose at the piano; "Lasca," a reading by Dick Hutchinson, and a Pantomime by Grace Smith. Now, that we've submitted to you a sample or two of what our various members can do, perhaps you would care to see how they look.

DRAMATIC CLUB

As this publication goes to press we find some of the group members busily engaged with the preparation of two short dramatic presentations, "The Other One" and "A Wedding."

Soon after this, commencement work will be started so that those who visit us then can say that our expressive spirit reflects the following thoughts:

"Oh, the thing that I call living isn't gold or fame at all!
It's good-fellowship and sunshine, and it's roses by the wall;
It's evenings glad with music, and hearth fire that's ablaze,
And the joys which come to mortals in a thousand different ways.
It is laughter and contentment and the struggles for a goal;
It is everything that's needful in the shaping of a soul."

Das Vereinlein

Sponsor...........Miss Emma Gillette
President.................John Hertz
Vice President. ....Gordon Powers
Secretary................Amy French
Treasurer...........Matilda Jupenlaz

AS VEREINLEIN, which roughly means "The Little Club," was organized the last semester of 1927-1928 under the sponsorship of Miss Emma Gillette. It was the first class of its kind in this college. Aside from promoting an informal interest in the German language, the club aims to stimulate phases of European life, customs and culture and to bring about a better understanding of the relation of these to our cosmopolitan world—a world that daily comes into closer communication with Europe. Das Vereinlein first made its successful appearance Stunt Night when, in a typical German Garden, its members presented a little glimpse of German life and customs.

The club is composed of students who have had one or more semester of German, and who have made grades sufficiently high to recommend them to the club.

Girls' Athletic Club

President...........Margaret Mannix
Vice President.......Mildred Williams
Secretary...............Frances Egan
Treasurer................Ruth Eisele

HE GIRLS' ATHLETIC CLUB is the largest and most important girls' club in the school—the only club with a definite objective of promoting and fostering girls' athletics. And those meetings! What member hasn't delighted in those eats—and coffee! Who hasn't enjoyed the programs and social hours? The Alabama Night Club, one of the big hits of the year, was directed by Miss Love, assisted by three of the club members. Though the benefits from this rollicking minstrel were small, they will be used to help foster athletics, both for club members and for those outside the club. The proceeds from last year's vaudeville show were spent to secure tennis rackets and shin-guards for those participating in the two most important girls' activities: tennis and field-hockey.

GEBalcom

Literary

PAUL R. MILLER
Editor

G.W. CASS
Faculty Advisor

ANTHONY SHELINSKY
Business Manager

ALLAN DOUGHTON
Assistant Editor

KENNETH HALSTEAD
Assistant Business Manager

The Carontawan

ITTLE NEEDS TO BE SAID OF THE WORK of the Carontawan Board. The results of their efforts are before you. What we have given you is the best that we could. We have not hesitated to follow in the traditional past when the ways of the past seemed best fitted for our purpose, nor have we kept from innovating anything that we thought would improve the calibre of our Annual. It seemed to us that Activities and Organizations overlapped and so we united them under Activities. Humor is being looked on with disfavor as a section in a year book and so instead of having a part of the book devoted to it we have omitted it, leaving the Diary of our year's work in its place.

The Board of the Carontawan is composed of twenty members who give their time in order to leave with the graduating class something to help recall the days spent in Mansfield. In a way it is a thankless task because no two would have it done alike, but on the other hand any little appreciation you may have for our work is the best form of remuneration that you may give us. We have tried to advance the standard of the Carontawan a little. We do not think it is near perfect, we expect a better work next year, and we hope that the next Board will be able to handle some of the problems that we found and have left unsolved; but if we have given you something that you are proud to own, something that you will want to keep, something that will bind you closer to Mansfield State, then we have succeeded.

J. BRIT DAVIS
Athletics

LOIS BALCOM
Art Department

HOWARD BURR
Organizations

ANOR PARKER
Assistant: Art Department

EDWARD AUGUSTINE
Assistant: Art Department

HILDA DAVENPORT
Assistant: Art Department

RUTH HUTHMAKER
Home Economics Editor

AGNES McCAUSLAND
Literary Editor

GUIDA MARROW
Assistant: Literary Editor

FRANK YURKEVITCH
Music Editor

AGNES McGROARTY
Humor

LLOYD STRAUGHN
Photographs

CARLTON JACKSON
Junior Representative

RUTH HOFFMAN
Freshman Representative

KENNETH DAYTON
Sophomore Representative

The Flashlight

OLUME FOUR of the Flashlight has been published by the students of Mansfield and that volume is now a thing of the past. It has been the privilege of the Flashlight to chronicle some of the most noteworthy events that ever happened at Mansfield during the past year and it has tried to present them in approved newspaper fashion. This has been hard to do as none of the board have ever had any experience or training along that line. Three of the past editors of the Flashlight assisted on the board and so helped get the paper going soon after the first week of school. The staff met with their traditional rivals, hard times, low

FLASHLIGHT BOARD

Standing: Burr, Smith, Jackson, Mannix, Williams, Kelly, Bennett, Miller.
Sitting: W. Davis, Beach, Dayton, Dr. Marshall, Doughton, B. Davis.

funds and all the rest of such hardships that beset as yet an unproven institution.
For the past four years the paper has slowly been evolving into what we hope some
day will be an established part of the school. This year added to the proof that the
Flashlight is a part of the student life that could not be well done away with.

The Flashlight has always followed the athletics of the school and given fair
and accurate accounts of the games. This year the paper was able to follow the
various teams through successful seasons. Much of the school spirit that backed the
teams so well was a result of the spirit the paper helped to create. The clubs and
organizations were all represented nearly every week. The aim of the Flashlight is to
print news of the school life of the students and has done this well. Some may say
that the paper is amateurish and takes in a small field. This is probably true, but it
fills a place here at Mansfield and therefore will no doubt live. Many outside agencies
tended to lower the circulation of the Flashlight this year. Other papers were formed
to handle news of various departments. This lowered the circulation, but not much.
There is no paper that handles news of the social life of Mansfield but the Flashlight.
The staff of the Flashlight deserves much credit for the work they spent on the paper.
There is little about the school that compares in drudgery to constant grinding out of
words when thoughts refuse to come and the copy is due at the printer's. Through the
work of the staff Mansfield has had a better insight into her school life and those
outside have had a chance to learn what a great place Mansfield State is after all.

Emersonian Literary Society

HE EMERSONIAN LITERARY SOCIETY was organized in 1914 to fill a gap that, incredulous as it may seem to us now, three other large literary societies could not fill. Literary societies at that time held one of the highest places in extra-curricular activities because of the attitude of both teachers and students toward them. The last fifteen years have witnessed many changes in the activities of colleges and universities, along with them is the attitude toward the literary society.

When our school changed from a State Normal to a State Teachers College, two fragments of literary societies existed. That spring the Athenaean Literary Society held its last meeting leaving the uncoveted field to the Emersonian, the youngest literary society in the school. Last year a few ambitious members and Dr. Elizabeth G. Marshall decided not to let the Emersonian Literary Society die the easy and natural death that many such organizations all over the land had died. The Emersonians realized that to organize and promote a literary society which would appeal to the present day college student they must set forth new aims and make the literary society an organization which would supplement and enrich the English courses in the school. The aims of the new society also carry out a program that will help graduates of Mansfield to organize and conduct collateral activities in their own teaching experiences. In looking over these two aims you will see that our society by carrying them out will meet "both the immediate and assured future needs" of its members. A society or club that accomplishes this does not need to fear an easy and natural death. This year we continue along the lines that were definitely planned last year. Probably the two greatest accomplishments of the year are the forming of a new constitution, with provision made for honors and credits. Six solid gold E's set with pearls will be given every year to the six members who receive the largest number of credits. Credits are given for scholarship, literary attainment and distinguished service in the college at large. The second, and by no means the lesser in importance, is the promotion of inter-collegiate debating.

Standing: Davis, Burgess, Bartoo, Krutzeck.
Sitting: Singer, Jones, Tozer.

Inter-Scholastic Debating Team

URING THE YEARS 1923 and 1924 Mansfield had Inter-Society debating teams composed of members of the Athenaean and Emersonian Literary Societies. The debate of '24 was won by the Athenaeans, who on the negative side held forth that "The Production and Distribution of Coal and Oil in the United States Should not Be Regulated by the Federal Government." While that of the preceding year was won by the Emersonians who brought to members of the college and proved that, "Organized Labor was not a Menace to Our Country." Then for a few years athletics ranked foremost in our college and interest in the literary field declined. Again the literary enthusiasm has appeared and as a result the Emersonians are sponsoring one of the important projects of the club and of the school. It has as its object the training of minds to think quickly, clearly and logically and, as has been proven, debating can perform this task much more efficiently than most other means.

When the "try-outs" were over and the team had been selected, the question arose as to what question should be debated. After "getting in touch" with Bloomsburg's team the question "Should the Present Jury System Be Abolished?" was selected. Next came the problem of finding suitable material and coaches. These were soon settled. The library has co-operated splendidly in securing much valuable material and making it accessible to the student of the debating team. As for coaches, Dr. Marshall, Mr. Webster, and Mr. Chatterton efficiently coached the team, obtaining very satisfactory results for a beginning adventure. The year 1929 holds for all students of Mansfield, the memory of that notable night of April 9th when Mansfield and Bloomsburg held out in argumentation upon the discussion of the subject, "Resolved, that Our Present Jury System Should Be Abolished."

Teacher Training Magazine

Faculty Sponsors—Myron E. Webster, George A. Retan.
Business Manager—Miss Evelyn Thomas.

UNDER THE DIRECTION and guidance of Professors George Retan and Myron Webster, the "Junior High School Quarterly" of last year has been expanded to include material having to do with elementary as well as Junior High school education. The new quarterly is published under the name, "Teacher Training Magazine." The primary object of this magazine is to aid in the training of teachers. In editing the various issues, an attempt has been made to give the subscribers the best possible insight into school problems and to keep them posted on the phases and methods of teaching in the various school departments. This has been done by articles, notes and book reviews, contributed by people already in the field, as well as our own students, which accurately and adequately picture the major and minor problems and solutions for them. It is not only the work in the class room that is discussed, but the extra-curricular activities as well are given unlimited space and comment. Through this medium the sponsors hope to stimulate the teacher in training to a keener zest for the work of teaching and an improved technique in the solution of its many problems. It is hoped that this magazine will continue to develop and to serve as a factor through which teachers in training may receive definite and worthwhile helps.

We have been fortunate in having as contributors of major articles to our magazine prominent workers in the field of education. In the issues of the "Junior High School Quarterly" of last year our major articles were written by men who have had actual experience in meeting and solving of real and vital school problems. Such men were: Mr. W. H. Bristow, Pennsylvania State Department of Public Instruction; Dr. Henry Klonower, Director of the Teachers Bureau at Harrisburg; George A. Retan Director of the Training School at Mansfield State Teachers College; Dr. Albert L. Rowland, Superintendent of Schools, Cheltenham District; Dr. Isaac Doughton, head of the Education Department of the Mansfield State Teachers College; Rock L. Butler, Supervising Principal, Wellsboro Schools; Dr. Belknap, Dean of Instruction, Mansfield State Teachers College; Hugh Alger, Supervisor of Science, Junior High School, Mansfield; Miss Jesse Grigsby, Supervisor of Mathematics, Junior High School, Mansfield.

We have been equally fortunate this year in securing fine articles written by such prominent educators as Dr. William R. Straughn, Principal, State Teachers College, Mansfield; A. P. Ackeley, Superintendent of Schools, Potter County; C. W. Lillibridge, Superintendent McKean County; Superintendent Morrow, Bradford County; Myron E. Webster, Principal of Junior High School, Mansfield; Miss Mildred Grigsby, Supervisor of Grade Six, Training School, Mansfield; Miss Lu M. Hartman, Department of Home Economics, Mansfield State Teachers College.

Social Activities

Freshman Frolic

True to the tradition established by Freshman classes, the class of '32 came out with one of the finest dances of the year. Of course, because of the fact that the affair was sponsored by Freshmen, many of the upperclassmen maintain that the affair was of an inferior degree of excellence as compared to those of other class hops. However, one has only to point to the decorations, music, or refreshments handed out by the various committees to dispel any doubt as to the subject in question.

The decoration committee, with Gomer Lewis as chairman, took it upon itself to make the best of the opportunity and advertise the college in general and especially the class of '32 by means of a few hundred, more or less, paper banners with a huge '32 printed thereupon, which were liberally distributed around the gym. Intrically interspersed with these were myriads of many-hued balloons, toward which longing eyes were continually gazing. As additional decoration there were distributed many packages of confetti and streamers which when used made a display of color that was most pleasing to the eye.

Nor was the pleasing of the ear less neglected. The famous Red and Blacks were at the helm and as is always the case when they preside, there was a brand of music produced which would make even the most indifferent of dancers to step out and enjoy himself to the utmost in following his program. And with the program, also, the Freshmen proved that they weren't "so dumb." The programs were of neat black leather, tied with a red cord. On the front was engraved the seal of the college, together with the name of the class and the dance. Last, but in no manner least, came the refreshments. The committee, with Jane Thompson at the head, brought in eats of a quality and quantity to refresh even the most jaded of the "hoppers" and make him wish that the dance would last all night. Of course, it was rather a disappointment to have the dance scheduled for the afternoon, but aside from that we are very well satisfied, to say the least. And now we wish to show our appreciation to those who made the dance possible, namely, committees, sponsors, officers, and orchestra. Come on, folks! Bottoms up!

198

Sophomore Hop

If one had elected to visit the M. S. T. *C.* gymnasium on the morning of last February sixteenth, he would have seen about twenty industrious Sophomores hustling and scurrying about like so many ants. If that same individual had visited that same gym at 6:45 that night, what a change would have greeted him. Hearts of all sizes transformed the barrenness of our basketball court into a softness and beauty is is not accustomed to. Gay streamers were strung from every place imaginable and back again. The decorations were surely a work of art. Fred Bennett, as chairman of the decorations committee, is a versatile man. He is an interior decorator, as well as a coming pedagogue.

As for the programs, they were just the thing. Howard Baker was chairman of this committee and —well—just take a glance at these good-looking programs.

The dance committee procured the services of our own inimitable Red and Blacks and how these boys did produce syncopation. Anyone with two feet could have "stepped about" to their trots, waltzes, blues, stomps, or what have you. Glenn Hammer, captain of the dance committee, did a hard job well, and that is satisfying 125 couples with one orchestra.

During intermission the Sophs and their guests made quick work of the punch and groceries served by the refreshment committee. Everyone had plenty and felt better for the second half. The favors, consisting of corsages and multi-colored pencils, went over big, as did the entire three hours. Julia Beaver, chairman of the committee, is a credit to the Home Economics department. Everyone who attended the hop will agree that she knows her refreshments.

A big slice of credit goes to Gaylord Spencer, our congenial president. "Doc" put a lot of time and work into the affair and he is to be congratulated on its success. For our chaperones we selected Dr. and Mrs. Straughn, Mr. and Mrs. Belknap, Dean Fischer, and Prof. Chatterton, the class advisor.

199

Junior Prom

Utilizing the season of tho Irish primate, all plans were laid to carry out the setting with the green and white shamrock. Saint Patrick could not aspire to higher fame than was tendered to him when on the eve of his recognition all Mansfield came tripping to his green standard. This was the showering of a surprising popularity upon the Junior class when the usual quota of programs failed to meet the demands of the pleasure seekers. Though it upset the order of plans, it was a rather pleasant result for the class. Filling in all gaps and completing all final arrangements, the stage was all set for the "gran' ole time."

On March 16, 1929, at 6:30 p. m., Mansfield was the scene of many hurried activities. It was the realization of the hopes of the class of '30 when the college gym was opened to the dancers, presenting a very appealing picture to the joyous congregation. The first impressions of the hall were lasting for besides offering a treat to the eyes, the pleasant rhythm handed across the stage was the fulfillment of any previous estimations. "The Arcadians" made their first appearance in the midst of Mansfield's light trippers and from the demonstrations of evident approval, the entertainers aptly supplied a variety and a quality in their program.

It was not just one of the ordinary dances, and those glad raggers enjoyed the best of times with the frequent addition of moonlight dances. In keeping with the spirit of the time, the refreshing fluid was green fruit punch, "open all hours," and "the drinks on the house." Though the only thing in refreshments, there was enough to keep the dancers well lubricated for the evening. Spirits ran high, while colored caps and small shamrocks were given as souvenirs and then came the end, but when the hour indicated the time for the breakaway, the merrymakers, with a noticeably slow gait, reluctantly left the gym, evidently expressing thoughts on one of the good old times to be remembered.

Senior Ball

Saxophone a-sobbing, sobbing in the dusk,
Mignonette and violet, ambergris and musk;
Violin a-wailing, like a soul in pain,
Paris, Lys, and sandalwood quickened by cocaine.
Drums a-beating cadence, neither slow nor fast,
Bringing all our old, old dreams winging from the past;
Strings that keep a-crying, horns that shrill and squeak,
And always that piano, thumping fine and sleek.
Gentle lights a-shining, shining in the night,
Dwellers in our own young world, forever sad and bright.

Charles Gray must have been looking ahead to our ball when he received the inspiration to write his little poem—it describes the Senior dance of 1929 to perfection. It was all he said and more, for how can mere words picture the excitement, glorious excitement long preceding the occasion, or tell of the envies and disappointments and the happy joy in being one of those to attend Mansfield's greatest social affair. Periodically throughout the year occur dances, proms and frolics, the college's social functions. As a grand climax to all these the seniors put on their annual ball. What a glamorous term. Yet meaning to us at Mansfield a multitude of pleasant memories.

And so went the dance. If an observer had been standing about the arcade on the evening of April 20, he would have seen an endless stream of humanity pouring into the gym from all points of the compass, for many of the old "grads" were back to participate in a modernized form of an age-old art. Girls in brilliant evening gowns escorted by men in faultless formal dress, made up the parade. On entering the gym, the decorations, all in pastel colors, greeted the merry-makers. Yes, and there on a cleverly decorated stage was "Eddie" Minnick's famous band. What a setting for a grand and glorious evening. And no one was disappointed or sorry for coming. The long drives, the nerve racking process of getting into an evening gown or Tuxedo was forgotten.

An instant's silence, and then at precisely seven-thirty, to the tune of thudding drums, the wailing of the clarinets and the screams of the flute, the seniors took possession of the Gym for their annual fracas.

Not to be outdone by the underclassmen, who had served excellent refreshments at their dances, the senior committee decreed that the seniors would put out a treat to be remembered. So the most excellent refreshments were served in the college dining room where groups had reserved tables and were served by waiters. Mrs. McKinney deserves much credit for the manner in which she co-operated with the committee in working out the refreshment problem.

No class in previous history has a chance to boast of such favors and programs as were presented at the Ball of 1929. They were unique and unusual and by far the best ever given at Mansfield. Just ask the girl who has one.

And so ended one of the events long looked forward to; one that has been annually observed and has become a part of the college's cherished traditions, the Senior Ball, a gala event in the life of the Mansfield collegian.

Open "M" Club Dance

Every year the Athletes of the college get big-hearted and tender the people at large a big time in the shape of a shindig of enlarged proportions. The gym was neatly and prettily decked in the traditional colors of Red and Black, with blankets strewn over the seats, exactly as they are scattered over the fields of gore. Music was supplied by Hackett's Pennsylvanians, and they, to say the least, did the job up brown. We hail our fellow warriors with all the honor, glory, and adoration that comes only with sacrifice for "The Little Town Upon the Hill."

Private "M" Dance

Although credit must be given for the open party the boys threw, it could not vie with the private party. Through quaint persuasion and persistent effort, the Junior High School gymnasium was secured to honor the existence of their organization. From the list of twenty orchestras bidding for the job, Oldfield's Quintet was selected, and justly so. The music was so hot, ice-water was served throughout the affair. A note of informality was struck in every phase, and although the dance was bred of dignity and exclusiveness, it did not prevent anyone from having a good time.

Y. W. C. A. Valentine

St. Valentine never was honored in such style as the Y. W. C. A. saw fit to fete him. The women used his trump card of hearts as the keynote of their decoration scheme, having the symbol of love arranged in as many forms as ingenuity permits. Don Baldwin's Band, dressed as Chinese, played a smooth job in complete harmony with the entire affair. Tea and cake touch a unique chord in the refreshment line. Summarily speaking the dance was all that could be asked.

Y. M. C. A. Dance

Keeping in accord with the dances at the Mountaineer institution is a hard task. Yet the Y. M. C. A., headed ably by Harry Summers, gave the college boys and coeds a real time, tempered only by the ceiling. The Arcadians, a combination school-boy and workingman outfit, came into the arena with all the powerful blend of good rhythm. Refreshments of punch and cake served to satisfy the thirsty palates. Simple but effective blue and white decorations, the symbolic colors of the national association, took much of the bareness away from the gym. Even if they do claim it was the best of the year, it was as good as any of them.

Music Supervisors' Party

What an enjoyable, delightful year for the Music Supervisors this has been! The most worthy Seniors and Juniors made a pilgrimage to the Steadman Rancho early in the fall when the trees of the forests 'round about displayed their vari-hued foliage. Despite the rain, inspections were made of the fields, the cattle, the barn and the orchards. (Ah, those delicious plums!) And then the girls set forth upon the table a veritable banquet fare, a juicy steak dinner fit for a king. In the guise of entertainers for the evening we found Miss Brooks, Mr. Myers and his colleagues Ringrose and Huston, and Boghdan Shlanta. Reluctantly, on the stroke of nine, we must bid our adieus and leave this bit of western life in the mountains of Pennsylvania.

Music Supervisors' Dance

The annual Music Supervisors dance, according to the custom carried out for the three past years, was sponsored by the Sophomore Supervisors on the eve of April 27th. With a Maypole and all its rainbow ribbons adorning the gym, one was reminded of Merrie England and ye olden time dances on the green. But, however, we preferred the present day gathering, the smooth, glassy dance floor, the slow, dreamy, moonlight waltzes, the gliding, langorous tango, and the speedy peppy fox trots. Who could resist dancing when such irresitible "danceable" music was played by the Arcadians? And then the ever-thirst-quenching punch bowl and dainty sweet only made it all sweeter. What could be sweeter, what could be more ideal than the balmy spring air, the perfect music, the ideal chaperones, and rainbows around every shoulder?

Soph Music Dance

The Sophomores, with Mr. and Mrs. Myers as sponsors, seem to have had quite a hilarious time this year. Early in the season they danced to the tunes plaved by the Arcadian Music Makers in the music assembly room. The "Salon" was artistically bedecked in holiday attire. Everyone present bedecked himself with the delicious refreshments at hand. The feature of the evening was an exhibition of dancing at Mansfield, given by the Misses Kunkle and Wendel. One evening in the spring, to be exact—'twas the first day of spring, the Sophs found their way to the House of Myers, where they feasted sumptuously and then spent the evening in playing cards, after which they must needs wend their weary way collegeward in the rain.

Frosh Music Dance

And the Freshmen! Ah, we must not forget our youngsters. They, too, danced in the Music Assembly Room one evening in December. With Mr. and Mrs. Hartman and Mr. and Mrs. Angus Steadman as sponsors and chaperones, with the Yuletide decorations of evergreen boughs, paper streamers and colored lights, with delicious refreshments, and with the music played by members of the Music Supervisors' Club, public opinion states that it was indeed a worthy affair.

203

Rurban Club

GROUP OF ENTHUSIASTIC young people who believe in a square deal for the country child and are working for better conditions in the rural schools—that's the Rurban Club. Miss Clara Winans first organized the club in 1923. A need was felt; a need that could partly be supplied by the active co-operation of a group that was in sympathy with the problems that face each country child attending a country school. A better educational horizon was supplied through the medium of books; and thus the traveling library of the Rurban Club came into existence. Of course, the five libraries that are in the field at the present time are inadequate to meet the demand made upon them, but we hope that this little work of ours will receive recognition from more powerful sources, and that these powers to be will endeavor to carry out our work to a fuller degree. There is no doubt about it. The club has grown steadily since its birth and we can safely say that, at the present time, is the strongest organization in the college.

Here is a brief story of what the club has done during the 1928-1929 term. The club started its term with a pan cake breakfast in Smythe Park. Here, amidst a spirit of merry-making, the members of the club became acquainted with each, other, discussed plans for the school year, and then began working. The meetings were called at once; a definite time being set aside each first and third Thursday of the month. Each meeting was made interesting by educative reports, musical programs, and social games.

The traveling libraries were sent to the school requesting them. One new library was purchased by the club and sent into the field this year. The club decided to lead out into a new project which consists of a large scrap book. The sheets of the new scrap book are to be filled with pictures and articles concerning the rural schools of Pennsylvania. Each member of the club is to have a sheet for his report to a rural school.

The large social event for the members of the club was Rurban Day, which was held in March. Lectures, the club luncheon, the county fair, and the play put on by the members of the club, were the features of the day.

The Art Club

First Semester	Second Semester
President............Matilda Jupenlaz	President.................Helen Felts
Vice President.............Iona Dawes	Vice President...........Helen Curtis
Secretary..:...............Ruth Tozer	Secretary................Erma Kelley
Treasurer................Martha June	Treasurer...............Helen Sharpe

FOUND IN THE SEVEN-FOLD LAW of the Camp Fire Girls is an aim which is fitting for the Art Club to follow: "Seek Beauty." Probably no person exists who does not love beauty in some form. There are some, however, who do not know how to express their inner impressions. So they grope blindly forward, dissatisfied because they cannot attain the goal for which they aim. The Art Club constantly endeavors to help its members to seek beauty and to find it in the everyday things about them. At several of the meetings faculty members have described their travels to foreign lands, and have emphasized in particular the beauties of great cathedrals—poems in marble and granite.

Yet the club does more than this. Through finely organized programs worked out by faithful members, and the capable sponsor, Miss Barnhardt, each member is taught that loveliness may be created from even the most commonplace things. In this way each person not only has the road to self-expression opened to him, but also he gains the ability to help others to do that which he can do.

So, to the first aim, "Seek beauty", let us add the second, "Give Service."

Hiking Club

"Robin Hood"—Gay laughter—"How about a little firewood?" "Any matches?" "U-um, sweet cider, weiners and rolls—say, who planned this feed anyway?" Good times like that one are plentiful when you belong to the Hiking Club. Not one of the band (including our sponsor) worries about a broken fingernail or a shiny nose. We believe in "a sane mind in a sane body." Our hikes keep us in good trim and our meetings are nothing if not promotors of "sane minds."

That the Hiking Club members believe in practicing their slogan, "Hike for Health," is evident when we see in their records that 18 members last year received numerals for hiking the required 250 miles. This year's numeral record promised to be even better. The additional 200 miles necessary for a Club Pin have been earned by several members this year.

"When better Hiking Clubs are made, Miss O'Brien will make them."

Outdoor Club

As the name signfies, this group of girls is composed of those having a keen interest in one thing—the out-of-doors. Their very purpose is to learn more about out-of-doors life through studying various types of plant, animal and bird life in this section. The club aims to undertake and complete some one project of practical value dealing with nature each year.

The members learn much about the surroundings in which they live, and in this way get a real joy in life. This satisfaction comes from learning to recognize wild flowers, describing their habitat and so far as possible, the family to which they belong. They learn to recognize the native birds, both by sight and sound, and all that is possible about these feathered friends. To complete the out-door training a systematic study of trees is made. Aside from the actual outdoor work, many books and poems dealing with nature are read and discussed.

The club has a regular meeting night at which time a business program and social gathering is held. Here the work of the individuals is brought together so that all may benefit by the work of each. The eats and play hold their place with the girls and come in for their share of consideration.

Any college girl who is interested in this type of work and who is willing to give some time to the club activities is eligible to membership. The membership is limited to forty members.

Willet McCord
Bass and Violin

David Gotwals,
First Sax, Clarinet.

George Wilson,
Second Sax, Clarinet.

Leonard Smith,
Trumpet.

Arthur Dawes,
Trombone.

Willis Oldfield,
Piano.

Arthur Covey,
Banjo.

Don Winship,
Third Sax.

George Palmer, Manager and Leader
Drums and Traps

Red and Black Serenaders

When life has turned our footsteps from these pleasant paths and led us far afield, surely the name, "Red and Blacks," will be instrumental in calling back the half forgotten memories of many pleasant social parties and friendships of our dear old Alma Mater. For many years an ever-changing group of musicians have taken this name, held the standards high and made this band the official dance orchestra of the school. The fame of this band is not at all local. It is known throughout the collegiate circle for miles around. Penn State, Albright, Cornell, and many other colleges have had their house parties and Frat dances enlivened and their success assured by the peppy syncopators from Mansfield. Hardly a week passes that does not see the "Buick" leaving the Arcade, piled high with musical instruments on the outside, and packed tight with the Red and Black personnel on the inside. Many of Mansfield's class functions have been recorded as a success because of the intangible something with which this band embues happiness into the minds of those present.

Arcadians

Gordon "Gord" Lloyd, Director...Reeds
Elmo "Hack" Hackett, Manager..Piano
Charles "Guzzle" Wilkinson......Reeds
Rudolph "Rudy" Corbett........Reeds

William 'Bill" Briggs..........Brass
Mitchell "Mitch" Woodhouse.....Brass
Charles "Chuck" Corbett......Strings
Blair "Smoke" Spencer........Drums

Once more Mansfield students find themselves in the glare of the spotlight. This time in the field of music. In 1925, Harry Swain, a former student of Mansfield, organized a band of players known as "The Arcadians." The organization came about when the Arcadia Theatre of Wellsboro found itself in need of snappy orchestra for pit and stage work. The band continued in this line for about two and a half years. At the end of this time the group was reorganized with Gordon Lloyd as director and Elmo Hackett as manager, the personnel remained the same. Since this time the Arcadians have gained a state-wide reputation as a "mean" dance orchestra, having been booked at many of the large eastern Pennsylvania theatres and colleges.

In Mansfield the Arcadians have held an equal rank with the famous Red and Black Serenaders. Many of the classes and organizations employing them to furnish the "pep" for their functions. The "M" Club, the Juniors, the Music Supervisors and the Y. M. C. A. never regretted having them on the bill at their annual dances. Each and every time they proved their right to the high reputation which accompanies the name "Arcadians."

Diary

September

10.—"Frosh" welcomed. Community sing in "gym."

11.—Bills paid thru mail, not so much delay before entering classes. Get-to-Gether dance.

12.—"Frosh" initiation at Cannon and in "well." A dance in "gym." Pajama party in "Y" rooms.

13.—Faculty reception.

14.—Dance and movies (Missing Link). There were a number, no doubt.

15.—"Frosh" initiation in S m y t h e Park. Musical entertainment and games. Dance. Puffed rice and molasses. Contest.

16.—Vespers. Dr. Straughn.

17.—Football fellows arise at 6 A. M. to start on a run for an hour. (Reasons unknown.) Baptist and Presbyterian receptions. (Where are the best eats? ? ? ? ?)

18.—First House meeting. Now things will be different.

19.—First Girls' "gym" dance. Episcopalian reception. Most everyone but Episcop's attended.

20.—Y. M. and Y. W. reception.

21.—Beginning of Fair (rainy) vacation.

22.—Prisoners left their cells and attended the fireworks at the Fair with the "Warden."

23.—Vespers. Dr. Straughn, speaker. Schlanta. violinist. Sperry, musical directress.

24.—Introduced "Frosh" to beloved dish—"Hash"! ! ! ! ! Football practice begins.

25.—Announcement of Orchestra's beginning by Dr. Butler. Rain. All ducks from the Collitch were seen in town.

26.—Grape season started. Watch out for the next couple of weeks.

27.—Radio concert in Y. W. rooms. Movies (In Old San Francisco).

28.—New hymn in Chapel (Mansfield). Dr. Butler told us something about chords in music. We'll all be music "soups."

29.—Football scrimmage. Dance—two orchestras. Bo Bo Four and Uneasy Seven. Y. W. Pancake-Sausage breakfast.

30.—Excitement galore—like all Sundays at Mansfield State Teachers' College.

October

1.—Dancing class. E v e r y o n e but "Frosh" must leave.

2.—Don Baldwin trying to get cheer leading squad together (boys and girls). Few cheers led by Tony Suhocke. How times have changed. Marge Gialdini and Ag. McGroarty were seen playing checkers in the "Y" rooms.

3.—Prizes coming from questionnaire. Cheers, fifteen girls leading; six boys. Some one didn't watch directions and yelled "Fight" by herself. Calisthenics by boys and girls cheer leaders to tune of football song. Grape sherbet.

4.—First meeting of board. No slivers were loose. Candlelight service in "Y" rooms.

5.—Play, at night, and dance. Music furnished by Uneasy Ten.

6.—First Rurban Club breakfast. Big game between Clarion, 0, and S. T. C., 20. Dance, music by Red and Blacks.

7.—Usual procedure. Shoe sale in N. H. Any shoes were to be found hung on the molding.

8.—Prevention Day. Demonstrations of first aid and life saving by Commodore Longfellow.

9.—Mental Health Day. During program at night entertainment by gallery gods, singing "Covered All Over With Snow."

10.—Personal Appearance Day. It's a good thing these days come once in a while.

11.—Personal A p p e a r a n c e Day. Snakes! "Y" hike to Robinhood.

12.—Pep(less) meeting.

13.—Parents Day. Susquehanna, 0, M. S. T. C., 40. Dance and concert.

14.—Edgar Frear and Grantley Cooke start counting blades of grass.. (Campused.)

15.—Hiking Club picnic to Robinhood.

16.—O Sole Mio, Mr. Manser (expression). Selection by orchestra.

17.—Athletic Club picnic to Oakwood Home. "X" visited Blossburg Hospital and treated by nurses. Bus load of students go to Elmira to see dancer.

18.—Hot rolls, Rubette ice cream. Rurban Club "Hick" party.

19.—Scotch Singers. Wellsboro High, 0, vs. Scrubs, 6. Frosh, 6, Sophs, 13.

20.—Lock Haven, 0, vs. M. S. T. C., 6. Dance, music by Uneasy Ten.

21.—Revival meeting at Vespers.

22.—Anne Flaherty called before council. Wonders will never cease.

24.—Paul Miller takes the part of Lincoln in giving Gettysburg Address, but he gives Carontawan address.

25.—Tony makes a few remarks about Carontawan. Class race for Carontawan. Pictures of Dempsey-Tunney fight at Y. W. Hallowe'en party.

26.—No one late for breakfast due to false alarm, saying Junior High on fire. Pep(less) meeting. Movies—"Sharp Shooters."

27.—Band and student body aecompany team to Cortland. School spirit exceptional. Hallowe'en party a "flop." Cortland, 0, M. S. T. C., 0.

28.—Rainy Sunday. Fewer parents than usual.

29.—Starting of mid-semester. Exams, exams and more exams. Dancing class (Freshmen girls only).

30.—Meeting of W. S. C. G. A. (Don't worry, gang, it only means a House meeting.) Milly Williams proctors, and falls asleep on steps studying for exams.

31.—Girl inmates gather on 7th and sing in celebration of Hallowe'en— Whoopee. Joint dance for one-half hour —Hallowe'en treat.

November

1.—Everyone wondered why Dean Balch's nose was swollen. Effects of night before. Someone hit him in the nose with a shoe. Dance on 5th—two-piece orchestra.

2.—Y. M. Minstrels.

3.—Oswego, 6, M. S. T. C., 7. Gavitt's first game. First team to score on us. First bonfire—out until 12:30.

4.—Band concert at Vespers. Thanks to Oswego fellows for taking our rope, now we may sleep a little later.

5.—Bishop Darlington speaks, but everyone was interested in watching Rev. Belt. Listen to final speeches until 10:30.

6.—Straw vote in C h a p e l. Miss Wheeler and Mr. Myers sing "O, No, John." Enjoyed by all.

7.—DAY OF DAYS. Everyone on time for breakfast. Fire drill. Formal dinner introduced—lasted until 7:10. Don't forget Frances Howard, Tony, Thomas and Jerry Gavitt, slow motion community singing in dining room instead of "well"—"Hail, the Gangs All Here," "Won't Get Home Until Morning," "How Dry I Am," and "Long, Long Trail."

8.—Pep meeting. Will the person who borrowed punch, please return it.

9.—Ned McCobb's Daughter by Miss Scureman.

10.—Bloom., 12, M. S. T. .C., 0. First defeat. Dance at night—five fellows, ??? girls.

11.—Armistice Day program at Vespers.

12.—No wonder classes started late in N. H., the elevator wasn't running and it took time to walk to sixth. Children's Book Week. Meeting of all students who eat in the college dining room at 6:45 Signed, Dr. Straughn. Three guesses why?

13.—Student from Senior High dances and does clicking with wooden sticks to advertise the operetta.

14.—Conference (when recess was given to the inmates on third floor) was held at Student Council meeting. Singing in the "well" after dinner.

15.—Dean Balch on duty after dinner sending fellows to Y. M.

16.—Dance, music by Pianathrope. Great time was had by all. If you don't know what hills are for, ask Shirey, Dobbie, Cooke, Frear.

17.—Dance in afternoon. Game, Ithaca, 0, M. S. T. C., 52. Bone crushers did their bit. "M" Club dance. Bonfire.

18.—Spring has come. Different ones were seen on the campus with coats. Not many up for breakfast. Why? ? ? Only plain bread for breakfast, Sunday's.

19.—New table assignments go into effect. Quiet? and how? ! ? ! ? Urban plays in the last quarter. We were all glad to see Mike Hrycenko saved by the "Sally's."

20.—Just a few more days before vacation.

21.—Thanksgiving dance, and singing at "well" at 10. Francis Shubert died 100 years ago. His birthday and Dr. Butler's was the same.

22.—Mr. Strait takes charge of Chapel.

23.—Homeward bound.

December

2.—Vacation over. Return of the "wild." Didja have a good time? Gee, I'm so tired; I wish we could rest for a day or so.

4.—All students were complaining of stiff necks due to holding their heads down too long for "grace" before meals.

6.—Another good joke. Mannix takes Sperry's place on the Council.

7.—Movies, "High School Hero."

8.—Concert and dance.

9.—Sunday—same as every other one. Church, meals, and quiet hour, but mostly quiet hour.

10.—Things were dull—so silly. Chamberlain went to Sociology class.

11.—It was plainly seen that the girls aren't used to the dark, because screams were heard in Alumni Hall, because the lights were out.

12.—Griffin, Moran, Lewis, and Joyce, the four horsemen, were campused.

13.—Griffin and Moran enjoyed lunch on campus instead of X trail. Y. M. and Y. W. joint meeting. Christmas program. Man from Fairmont State Teachers' College spoke.

14.—Christmas in the distance. Tree in front of N. H. lit. Y. W. Jitney dance. Faculty take-off. Parsons as Dr. Marshall and Fox as Pandora were exceptionally well.

15.—Y. M. dance. Student Council on a rampage. Students do not loiter in the Reception Room nor slam doors.

16.—Unusual Sunday. Romeo was lost without Juliet since he was socialed. He spent the day counting blades of grass on the campus.

17.—Chirping was heard in N. H. at 5:50 for the first around the "well" to celebrate the approach of Christmas.

18.—Three more days before vacation. Whoopee! ? ! ? ! ? ! ?

19.—Ellsworth Allis was asked what was a Mosaic. Mosaic is where varnish put inside the wall so that it won't be on the outside.

20.—Christmas party. Whoopee! ? ! ? ! ? Turkey! ? ! ? Turkey! ? ! ? When dreams come true.

21.—Singing at "well" at 6:30. Very pleasing program. Girls held a jail parade as it were and sang "Power"! ? ! ?

24-25.—Red and Blacks play in Wilkes-Barre. Little old reunion.

January

2.—Few return. Get-together dance.

3.—Chapel looked deserted. Too much vacation.

4.—Still dead. Flu epidemic.

5.—First basketball game. We won.

6.—Nothing anymore exciting than usual.

7.—Cold. Br-r-r-r. The first day we've seen the students step lively to classes.

8.—Red Letter Day for all. New privileges and rules announced for upper classmen. Cards into effect.

9.—Cards initiated at 4 P. M. by Mannix, Williams, Chamberlain, and Sperry.

10.—Boghdan Shlanta violin recital. Entertain for students in Model School.

11.—Athletic Club vaudeville. And how we did raise Whoopee and Hey Hey. We tried to do our bit.

12. Lock Haven, 14, vs. M. S. T. C., 54.

13.—Same as usual—church, quiet hour, vespers, and Sunday walks.

14.—Too cold to even sing the second song in Chapel.

15.—Dr. Straughn and Dean Belknap observe student teachers.

16.—Very, very unusual Pep! ? ! ? meeting. Marching around "gym" singing "Mansfield, Hail."

17.—Mrs. Royle from State College speaks to us. Something concerning prohibition.

19.—End semester. Bills being paid for rest of year.

21.—Mid-Semester d a n c e. "Coming Thru the Rye" exhibition by Irving T. Chatterton.

22.—New semester b e g i n s. What classes are you going to take? ? ? ? ? I don't want any on Saturday.

23.—Presented dinner tickets to get into the dining room.

24.—Pep(less) meeting.

25.—Wakely entertainment.

26.—Dickinson Seminary, 20, M. S. T. C., 24.

27.—Same as usual.

28.—Ground covered with snow. Many faw down and go boom.

29.—Per usual, a House meeting. There will also be a men's meeting.

30.—Inevitable Girls "Gym" dance.

31.—Matinee.

February

1.—Lock Haven, 19, vs. M. S. T. C., 44. Dance in "gym."

2.—Ground hog sees shadow. W. S. C. G. A. gives tea for students. "Hokus Pokus," mid-winter show of "M" Club.

3.—Nothing unusual for Sunday—church, quiet hour, and vespers.

4.—Coasting great on the campus.

5.—Elvidge, Yurkevitch, and Novak, grassed indefinitely. Good thing there was snow on ground to amuse them.

6.—What caused so many students to come late for breakfast? From the rush it looked like a sale. Dr. Straughn said "Everyone.must be there 7 minutes after 10."

7.—More on time for breakfast.

8.—Mannix birthday. Band in Chapel. Pep meeting. Bucknell, 22, vs. M. S. T. C., 36.

9.—Y. W. dance. Japanese affect.

10.—Unusual Sunday—chicken for dinner.

11.—Mr. Chatterton and Miss Jupenlaz hold hands coming out of dining room. Big day for following: Elvidge, Yurke, Novak, Simpson, and Baker, off campus.

12.—Lincoln's Birthday. Orchestra played "Around the Campfire" to celebrate. Hall meetings at 9. Girls on each floor given chance to show talent.

13.—Athletic Club meeting. Very pleasing program and dance followed.

14.—St. Valentine's Day. This must be the reason why we had hot rolls for breakfast. Scotch Love Songs played by orchestra . Pep meeting.

15.—Band in Chapel. Pep meeting. Irish Folks songs. Bloomsburg, 40, vs. M. S. T. C., 41.

16.—Soph. hop.

17.—Fair and warmer.

18.—Looked like first day of Spring.

19.—Fooled—snowed all day. Big night for students who attended H. S. play. Out until 11.

20.—Oriental rug display.

21.—Joint "Y" meetings—songs, etc.

22.—Washington's Birthday. Movies and dance.

23.—Bloomsburg, 24, vs. M. S. T. C., 39. Piano recital. First girls' basketball game, Frosh.-Soph. Parade downtown.

24.—Same as usual. Band at vespers.

25.—Fair and warmer.

26.—Spelling bee. Why the grand rush from the "well" when a certain table is dismissed?

27.—What causes Dean Belknap and Dr. Straughn to sit with student body when we sing "All For You?"

28.—Dr. Getty from Chicago speaks.

March

1.—Elizabethtown, 25, vs. M. S. T. C., 43. Movies, "When a Man Loves."

2.—Rurban Day. West Chester, 21, vs. M. S. T. C., 22. Rurban plays. Recital, piano and voice.

3.—Probably fair and warmer, possibly cold and rain.

4.—Inaugural address.

4.—Victory parade at 3. Classes dismissed. Victory dance, 4-5. Hammer shows talent by playing trumpet while dancing.

5.—Mysterious lunch. Where did apples disappear?

6.—Y. W. take charge of Chapel exercise.

7.—Once more students hurry to Chapel due to cold spell. Ask Papadick how the squashed cream puff felt in his pocket! ... .

8.—Dean Fischer takes charge of Chapel. "Alice, Where Art Thou" sounded weak due to not many present who were 40 years of age. Announcement—Vesper services Sunday evening will be under the orchestra. Schubert quartet.

9.—Frosh tea for upper classmen. Dickinson, 13, vs. M. S. T. C., 26. Big time in the Collitch. Dance after game until 10.

10.—Orchestra had charge of vespers.

11.—After singing "John Brown's Baby Had a Cold Upon His Chest" you'd imagine there were lots of babies around the school.

13.—Frosh, 16, vs. Sophs., 19 (girls game). More pep than big games.

14.—EXAMS are started. New slide at Collitch—Potato Slide. Waiters faw down and go boom.

15.—Downtown women students asked to leave Chapel, and Mr. Cornish makes his exit. "The Wedding" and dance at night.

16.—Junior Cotillion—more darn fun.

17.—Easter cantata at vespers. Irish Christmas.

18.—Frosh., 14, Sophs., 16 (girls game.)

19.—In Spring a young man's fancy turns to love. It shows our fellows aren't back on this because many are seen walking with their girls.

20.—Heard, "Gee, I'm glad vacation is near on hand. It will give us a chance to rest."—Jox's. Now I'll tell one.

21.—Big Easter dinner and dance, also quiet hour.

22.—Vacation Days. Exams still going strong.

22.—Homeward bound. How can I leave thee?

23.—April 1st—Vacation. The local lads teach school.

April

1.—Return. Many are fooled.

2.—6:45-7:45, debate in Chapel.

3.-4.—Lecture, Dr. Koischevitz.

5.—Play Town Clubs, 8, Senior H. S.

6.—German Day. They sure beat the Dutch!

8.—Allan Doughton takes his medicine every two hours instead of twice a day. The Dr. says he will live.

9.—Debate Nite, Blossburg.

12.—Mrs. Margaret Steadman—Doings in "gym" at 2 for. Movies. "M" Club dance in Hut.

13.—Waiters' party. Y. W. and Y. M. entertainment and dance to raise money for Eagles Mere.

18.—Rurban and Dramatic Club. Entertainment, Music Rooms.

19.—Emersonian play—Dr. Marshall.

20.—Senior dance, 7 to 11:30.

21.—Entertainment course. Vespers.

22.—Better Homes Week. Home Economics charge of Chapel.

26.—Movies.

27.—Baseball. Band contest in afternoon. Soph. music—Supr. Dance, 6:45 to 9:30.

May

1.—Baseball (away)—Cortland.

4.—Baseball (home)—Cortland. Mr. Myer's band concert and banquet.

8.—Baseball (away)—Bloomsburg.

10.—Mrs. Steadman's concert.

11.—Baseball (home)—B u c k n e l l. Council picnic (Watkins Glen).

15.—Baseball (away).

18.—Baseball (home)—Bloomsburg).

21.—Dress rehearsal.

24.—Photoplay at 8.

25.—General Alumni m e e t i n g, 11. Alumni dinner, 1:30. Baseball (home). Class reunion, 2:30.

26.—Baccalaureate, 10 A. M. Band concert, 3 P. M. Orchestra concert, 7:30 P. M. Music by faculty.

27.—Senior Class Day exercises. Senior play.

28.—Commencement, 9:30 a. m. That's all. There ain't no more.

*Advertising is the sugar
that sweetens business*

You will find the gang at the

X-Trail

Where You Get the Good Eats
Where You Will Feel at Home

Appreciation of Your Patronage
Is Expressed In Service Rendered

Mr. and Mrs. Burt Cheesman

I Am Photography!

I turn back the pages of the Book of Memory. I bring you Thoughts of Past Years and Old-Time Friends. I keep forever Green the Happy Hours of Childhood. I dull the Pangs of Bereavement and blunt the Edge of The Grim Reaper's Scythe. I carry the News of the World, and bring you Visions of Far Distant Lands. Our modern Civilization is largely dependent on my efforts. Though Men may Pass and Empires crumble to Dust, my Magic will preserve their Likeness for Future Generations. Not Purse-proud, I am within the Reach of All. I solve Mysteries impenetrable to Mortal Eyes; I ferret out the Criminal when other Means have failed. I illumine the Pages of History, and make Learning Possible for the Multitude. Born instantaneously in a Ray of Light, I become Everlasting. As necessary in War as I am in Peace, I am Man's Servant, and yet his Master. I am an Art—and yet a Business. I am Photography.

54 WEST MARKET ST
WILKES-BARRE, PA.

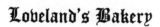

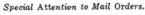

Building A College Annual

Is a big undertaking in any college. Especially is this true in a small college like Mansfield where the demands are for a standard of quality equal to the larger colleges. The Carontawan has always been just a little better than is expected in a school of this size.

We have enjoyed working with the various boards since the Carontawan was started, and we have been pleased to have had some part in making the Carontawan the book it is today. We have been glad to render that little extra service that has enabled the boards to make the Carontawan just a little better.

We would like to remind you that the extra service we have been able to give the Carontawan is typical of the service we make a part of our business practice, and we shall hope to serve you in any of your future needs.

Mansfield Advertiser